JOURNEY INTO INTERCESSION

A Practical Exploration of

What the Bible Says about Intercessory Prayer

Eric W. Bolger

Journey into Intercession: A Practical Exploration of What the Bible Says about Intercessory Prayer

Printed in the United States of America

ISBN 978-1-4303-1296-3

www.lulu.com

This book is dedicated to Dr. Robert E. Webber, whose example, encouragement and vision have impacted me more deeply than I can describe.

Acknowledgements

This book is the result of much input. Jennifer Freeman provided tremendous support as the book took shape, from the original concept to its fleshing out in study and writing. Her eye for realistic application of biblical teaching is a great gift, the marks of which are apparent throughout this book.

Thanks also to the women in Jennifer's "Women after Christ's Heart" (WATCH) small group at College of the Ozarks: Kelly Birch, Glory Borne, Stacie Davenport, Angela Ellett, Kristan Hammond, Laura Hanschu, Amy Kowalski, Ginger Langford, Sara Lee, Liberty Long, Brie Menjoulet, Natalie Perrigo, Jessica Richards, Janelle Richardson, Paula Senter and Christian Woelk.

Dr. Carla Waterman read through and provided excellent suggestions and guidance on the original thesis manuscript. Her support and encouragement are an ongoing blessing to me.

Many colleagues read portions of this book and gave valuable feedback, much of which is represented in this version. Special thanks to Floyd and Sarah Benda, Dr. Gary Hiebsch, Joanna Hubbard, Mark Kelley, Dee Klein, Dr. Mark Rapinchuk and Martha Smith.

John H. Sailhamer, who advised my Ph.D. dissertation work at Trinity Evangelical Divinity School, helped me see the beauty and majesty of Scripture, and more importantly of the God who stands behind it.

Kate Corley created the wonderful cover artwork based on her careful and faithful reading of the manuscript. Maren Nelson Rose helped transform Kate's work into a form usable for the cover.

Finally, my wife Janet, and children Andrew, Dan and Mark, are a constant encouragement to me in my professional endeavors. I could not do what I do apart from their generous support and friendship.

Any errors or omissions are solely the responsibility of the author.

May God use this book to his glory.

Contents

Day 2
Abraham and Lot (Genesis 18:16-33)

Day 3
Abraham and Abimelech (Genesis 20)

Day 4
The Servant of Abraham and a Wife for Isaac (Genesis 24)

Day 5
Moses and Pharaoh (Exodus 8:1-15, 20-32; 9:13-35; 10:1-20)

Day 6
Moses and Israel in the Wilderness (Exodus 15:24-25; 17:1-7)

Day 7
Moses and the Golden Calf, Part 1 (Exodus 32:1-14)

Day 8
Moses and the Golden Calf, Part 2 (Exodus 32:15-35)

Day 9
Moses and the Golden Calf, Part 3 (Exodus 33-34)

Day 10
Moses and Israel (Numbers 11)

Day 11
Moses and Miriam (Numbers 12)

Day 12
Moses and Israel (Numbers 14)

Day 13
Moses, Aaron and the Levites (Numbers 16)

Introduction

Welcome to the *Journey into Intercession*! The goal of this journey is a deeper understanding of intercessory prayer in the bible, an understanding that leads you to pray more effectively for others. On the journey, you will read and pray through many passages in the Old and New Testaments. You will also gain a deeper understanding of what the bible teaches about intercessory prayer. The passages are organized into daily devotional exercises, which should take anywhere from 15-30 minutes to complete.

What is Intercession?

Simply put, intercession is a specific type of prayer in which we pray for others. We may contrast it with petition, in which we pray for ourselves, and with prayers of confession, praise, and thanksgiving, which focus respectively on mending our relationship with God, honoring him, and expressing gratitude.

There is a broad range of "others" prayed for in the bible. There are prayers for loved ones and enemies, for believers and non-believers, for strong rulers and the weakest members of society. Biblical characters pray to a God who, though not visibly present, has promised always to be with us and to respond to our requests. Sometimes, most notably in the four gospels, this God *is* visibly present in the person of Jesus Christ. We see in these cases a fascinating picture of intercession, in which people bring others to Jesus to ask him to intervene in their lives. An example is the Canaanite woman in Matthew 15. This woman came to ask Jesus to heal her demon-possessed daughter, and Jesus responded positively to her request. In these types of accounts, we see intercession as the simple but profound act of bringing someone to Jesus for help. Not surprisingly, the results can be quite extraordinary!

Once again, we may define intercession simply as praying for others. In praying for others, we are bringing them before God himself and asking him to respond to their particular needs.

Why a *Journey into Intercession*?

Most Christians understand that conversation with God, which we commonly call prayer, is an essential part of their relationship with God. Most also understand that this conversation can take a variety of shapes and forms. There are times for adoration, times for confession, times for thanksgiving, times for asking, and times for simple companionship. All of these times fit broadly into a pattern of conversation that marks any serious relationship.

Journey into Intercession is designed to explore one aspect of this conversational relationship. Praying for others has a long and wonderful history in the bible, a history of which we do well to take note and emulate. Our journey through this rich history will begin in Genesis and end in the book of Revelation. Along the way we will study all the significant passages in the bible that deal in any way with praying for others. By the time we finish the journey, we will see the value that God places on our relationship with him, and the way he responds to our prayers for others.

Key Landmarks on the *Journey into Intercession*

When we survey the biblical landscape of intercession, seven key principles stand out. These principles provide landmarks for us along the journey, highlighting what is central to biblical teaching about intercession. We may summarize these landmarks with these words: **Relationship, Mediation, Character, Glory, Holy Spirit, Faith**, and **Thanksgiving**.

Principle One: Relationship

*Effective intercession grows in the soil of a deep and personal **relationship** with God.*

One cannot read the accounts of biblical intercessors such as Abraham, Moses, and Paul, and not be impressed with the depth of their relationships with God. These characters clearly wove intercessory activity into the cloth of this relationship.

Abraham is a great example. In Genesis 18, God tells Abraham that he may destroy the cities of Sodom and Gomorrah. This information leads Abraham to challenge God's justice, if he were to destroy the righteous along with the wicked in those cities. Conversing personally and boldly, Abraham "bargains" God into agreeing not to destroy the cities if there are ten righteous persons there. Such candid conversation with the God of the universe is striking, and draws us to consider the nature of the relationship between Abraham and God. Similar conversations mark the relationship between God and other biblical characters such as Moses, Hannah, David, Elijah, Mary, and Paul.

We will discover on this *Journey into Intercession* that God has established a deeply personal relationship with *all* of his children, and that this relationship is the context in which intercession is to occur. We never see Abraham or Moses praying to an impersonal and distant force. Instead, we see these men conversing with God as with a friend. Events happen or information is shared that elicits a concerned response from these faithful ones, and they immediately talk with God, not as one would talk with a stranger but as one would talk with a trusted companion. They speak with candor, unafraid to challenge God's plans or to argue with him. They are motivated not by fear but by a sense of acceptance that makes them confident of God's willingness to hear them out without retribution or anger.

Prayer is therefore an expression of relationship. Walter Brueggemann writes colorfully that prayer is "a way of participating in the covenantal dance."[1] This covenantal dance is the relationship God has initiated and sustains with his people. Effective intercession builds on this foundation of intimacy with God. One of the key things an intercessor must cultivate is a deep, personal relationship with God.

Principle Two: Mediation

*Effective intercession **mediates** God's blessings to others.*

A mediator is one who stands between two people or groups of people. The role of an intercessor is to stand between God and others, and to ask God to respond to the needs of others. The intercessor is a mediator.

We see this role of mediator most clearly in the biblical model of a priest. Beginning with Melchizedek and continuing through the rest of Scripture, priests are those who mediate the relationship between God and others. For example, a priest in the Old Testament would offer sacrifices to God on behalf of others. He would also communicate to them God's forgiveness and blessing. Significantly, when God made a covenant with the nation of Israel, he called them not only to *have* priests, but to *be* a "kingdom of priests" (Exodus 19:5-6). In this role the Israelites would be God's means of mediating between himself and other nations.

What exactly were the Israelites to bring to other nations on God's behalf? When God made a covenant or agreement with Abraham, he told Abraham that Israel (the descendents of Abraham) would be his means of restoring his blessing, lost at the fall, to all of humanity. That is, Abraham and his descendents would be the means by which God would bless all nations (Genesis 12:3).

The apostle Peter applies this analogy to the church. He uses the imagery of Exodus 19 to describe the calling that belongs to all believers in Christ. He tells them they are "a royal priesthood, a holy nation, a people belonging to God, that you may declare the praises of him who called you out of darkness into his wonderful light" (1 Peter 2:9). As a royal priesthood, believers in Christ now play the same role Israel did in the Old Covenant, serving to mediate God's blessings to the nations. Of course, the church is simply carrying out the ministry exemplified perfectly by Jesus. The author of Hebrews calls Christ the "mediator of a new covenant" (Hebrews 9:15). As Christ mediated the blessings of the new covenant while he was on earth, so now he has left the church with the same task, to mediate God's blessing to the world.

As mediators, those who intercede ask God to bless those for whom they pray. For example, Abraham prayed for God to heal Abimelech (Genesis 20), Job prayed for God to forgive his so-called friends (Job 42), and Jesus prayed for the crowds crucifying him not to have their sin held against them (Luke 23:34). The concept of a mediator helps us understand the task of intercessory prayer.

Principle Three: God's Character

*Effective intercession appeals to God's **character**.*

One of the most important lessons we learn on the *Journey into Intercession* is that it is not our character but God's that determines the effectiveness of our prayers. The negative side of this is that we really have no personal basis on which to appeal to God because, whether or not we realize it, we are quite pitiful creatures, full of sin and deception. Thus to approach God as if we have earned his help is a grave error. The positive side is that God is perfect in his character, and we can therefore depend on him to respond in a manner consistent with that character. In addition, this perfect character of God includes attributes such as mercy and forgiveness, compassion and unfailing love, patience and faithfulness. Thus, for example, it is appropriate to appeal to his mercy when others are in need of it because it is his very character to show mercy.

On the *Journey into Intercession* we will learn much about God's character, and about how biblical characters appeal to this character. All of the effective intercessors in the bible understand the God to whom they pray, which is not surprising in light of what we've already seen about the importance of the intercessor having a deep relationship with God. They consistently appeal to attributes such as his compassion, justice, love and mercy. They also appeal to his faithfulness, that is, the fact that he always keeps his promises. This character trait is especially important for intercession, because throughout Scripture God not only reveals his character but also makes promises to his people.

Paul understood well the relationship between God's character and his promises. Throughout Paul's prayers of intercession, which are some of the most powerful in all of Scripture, he first thanks God for what God has done for those Paul is praying for. For example, Paul thanks God for saving them, forgiving them, empowering them, delighting in them, and giving them hope. Then Paul appeals to God to continue supplying these things in even greater measure, *just as he has promised.* Since God is faithful, that is, true to his word, Paul knows this is an appropriate way to appeal to God's character.

Appealing to God's character and promises is essential to effective intercession. It is God's goodness, not ours, that gives us confidence in his response. When we learn to pray according to God's character and promises, we can be confident God hears and responds because it is his very nature to do so.

Principle Four: God's Glory

*Effective intercession flows out of a concern for God's **glory**.*

One of the things intercessors must always keep in mind is that the primary reason God responds to our requests is not our happiness but his glory. For example, Paul often prays that believers in Christ will experience the fullness of what God intends for them. This fullness includes deep and abiding hope, an awareness of their value in God's eyes, and the power God supplies for living in this world. These things are not, however, ends in themselves intended to make our lives better. Instead, God gives us these things so that we might display his character in our lives in a way that draws others into a saving relationship with him. God's answers to our prayers of intercession serve to show a spiritually hungry world that our God *is* the answer to its deepest needs and longings. In this way, God brings glory to himself through his answers to our prayers.

Moses understood this principle. Moses prayed that the plagues God sent on Egypt would help the Egyptians to see that the God of Israel is the one true God. The Egyptians had a distorted understanding of God, believing there were many gods over the various forces of nature. Through the plagues on Egypt God exhibited his true nature as the Lord of all creation, subject to no one and to no other god. The plague of darkness, for example, demonstrated God's lordship over the day and the night, and directly challenged

Egyptian beliefs. The concern Moses showed for God's glory will characterize all effective intercession.

A concern for God's glory flows naturally out of a deep, personal relationship with God. The better we know him, the more we realize that he is what life is really all about. What we thought were real needs pale in the light of God's glory. When we reach this place of living only for God, we join a host of other men and women in the bible and through history. We, like they, are concerned for God's glory rather than our own needs. Our prayers for others will reflect this priority.

Principle Five: The Holy Spirit

*Effective intercession depends on the work of the **Holy Spirit**.*

The bible clearly teaches that the Holy Spirit is essential to the ministry of intercessory prayer. As early as Numbers 11, we see the need for Spirit-empowered mediators in Israel. In this passage, when some Israelites complain about the unsanctioned prophesying of Eldad and Medad, Moses utters these memorable words: "I wish that all the LORD's people were prophets and that the LORD would put his Spirit on them!" (Numbers 11:29) Moses understands that the Israelites can accomplish their role as mediators only if God distributes his Spirit universally among them.

In Romans 8, Paul describes the way the Spirit intercedes for God's people in "groans that words cannot express" (8:26). The intercession of the Holy Spirit helps us in our weakness. Elsewhere Paul exhorts believers to "pray in the Spirit." He means, first, to pray in reliance on the Holy Spirit and not on our own strength, insight or wisdom. Second, and related to this, Paul means to pray with awareness that we live our lives in the context of an unseen but ever so real spiritual realm. To pray in the Spirit, then, is to seek the help of the Spirit, who not only strengthens us but also guides us to pray according to what is most true and real. "To Paul, prayer is ultimately the indwelling, energizing Spirit speaking with God himself."[2]

Reliance on the Holy Spirit is reliance upon God. Effective intercession requires such reliance. Intercessors must realize that they cannot accomplish spiritual work apart from the Holy Spirit. They must also realize that as they learn to listen to the Spirit, he will guide them as to how and what to pray. Many of the exercises in the *Journey into Intercession* invite readers to listen to what God would have them pray.

Principle Six: Faith

Effective intercession requires faith.

Faith, whether mentioned explicitly or not, is always central to the biblical passages dealing with intercession. We see the importance of faith for intercession most clearly in the gospels. Jesus typically highlights the faith of those who bring others to him for healing and help.

Why is faith so important? There are a number of answers to this question, though all of them enter into an area of mystery concerning God's sovereign control and our responsibility. Simply put, God has made the sovereign choice to invite humans into the process of accomplishing his will. Rather than simply ordaining what he wants to happen, he often uses human agents to carry out his purposes. Faith is one way he has invited us into the process. Faith is a way of expressing our dependence on him.

On the *Journey into Intercession*, we will see that God himself is the object of our faith. We have already noted the importance of appealing to God's character and promises. It is easy, however, when we pray for others, to place our faith in a particular result rather than in God's character. For example, if we pray for physical healing for someone, it is natural to assume that a successful healing is evidence that we had faith. We must place our faith not in a particular result but instead in the character of the God to whom we pray. We pray to God for healing because he is merciful. When we appeal to his mercy we can be confident he hears and responds, *whether or not the one for whom we are praying experiences healing.* It can be difficult to distinguish our confidence in God's character from confidence in a particular result, but it is a vital distinction for intercession. God is free to display his merciful character in any way he pleases. He will always show mercy, however, for this is his character.

One of the great prayers we will learn along the *Journey into Intercession* is this: Lord, I do believe, help me overcome my unbelief (see Mark 9:14). This prayer, uttered to Jesus by the father of a demon-possessed boy, is a great reminder of the difficult but necessary role of faith in our intercession. God can work with small faith, and an essential part of that faith is the recognition that we cannot have faith apart from his help.

Principle Seven: Thanksgiving

Effective intercession occurs in the context of thanksgiving.

Intercessory prayer and thanksgiving go hand in hand. This is true because, as we have already seen, effective intercession appeals to God's character and promises. Thanksgiving is how we express our gratitude to God for exhibiting his character in our lives, and for keeping his promises. Therefore giving thanks to God provides a natural context for praying for others.

Although we see intercession and thanksgiving linked throughout the bible, nowhere is the connection between the two as obvious and strong as in the prayers of Paul. In his letters, Paul typically prefaces his prayers for his readers with expressions of gratitude to God for what he has done on their behalf. For example, in Ephesians he begins by telling his readers how he thanks God for them:

> For this reason, ever since I heard about your faith in the Lord Jesus and your love for all the saints, I have not stopped *giving thanks* for you, remembering you in my prayers.

Then he prays for his readers:

> I *keep asking* that the God of our Lord Jesus Christ, the glorious Father, may give you the Spirit of wisdom and revelation, so that you may know him better. (Ephesians 1:15-17; emphasis mine)

The pattern of thanksgiving followed by intercession is so prominent in Paul's letters that it is clear that it was more than a mere formula. It was, in fact, an expression of his theology or understanding of God. The God to whom we pray is the same one who has begun and will complete a good work in those for whom we pray. To give him thanks for what he has done is a natural preface to asking him to do more of the same.

The church has typically made the connection between intercession and thanksgiving in its worship. Worshipers offer intercessory prayers during the celebration of the Lord's Supper. The Greek word for the Lord's Supper, *eucharisteo*, actually means, "give thanks." In the Eucharist, the worshiping community offers thanks to God for his work on their behalf. At the same time, it offers intercessory prayers.

The biblical connection between intercession and thanksgiving also reminds us that intercession is not simply an individual activity. It fits naturally in the context of corporate worship, during which the congregation joins to give thanks to God. Thus on the *Journey into Intercession* we will see the importance of the corporate side of intercession.

Some Dangers on the *Journey into Intercession*

Along with the positive examples in Scripture, we also have negative ones. In the *Journey into Intercession* we will come across a number of attitudes and practices that can be detrimental to intercession and to the spiritual life in general. These include related dangers such as spiritual complacency and arrogance, spiritual elitism and dumbing down. They also include incorrect understandings of prayer, such as manipulation.

Spiritual complacency and *spiritual arrogance* are really two sides of the same coin. Complacency in prayer is sometimes due to a view of God's sovereignty and control that seems to make prayer unnecessary. Why pray if God is going to take care of things anyway? The opposite side of the coin is what we can call spiritual arrogance. This is the attitude that God cannot and will not accomplish his purposes unless we pray. Both views fail to take into account the tensions and mystery that characterize biblical prayer. We have already seen that God has freely chosen to invite us into a relationship. In this relationship, he gives us the responsibility and privilege of having an impact on the outcome of events. Douglas V. Steere, in his book *Dimensions of Prayer*, helps us to see how God's sovereignty and our responsibility in prayer can go hand in hand. He observes that "God's ultimate purpose is unchanging, but . . . his strategy may vary infinitely."[3] If this is the case, Steere reasons, then it should not surprise us that God will vary his strategy in response to a believer who, through prayer, expresses confidence in this ultimate purpose. God is sovereign, but this sovereignty does not negate our impact. It actually provides a context for us to play a significant role. Unless we understand this, we can easily fall into the extreme of complacency or arrogance.

Spiritual elitism and *spiritual dumbing down* are also two sides of the same coin. The spiritually elite view themselves as more mature than other believers, and this attitude becomes a source of pride. Those who promote spiritual dumbing down believe that there is no difference in spiritual maturity among believers – all are equally mature and capable of leading others. Once again, both sides are in error. The fact is that there are different levels of spiritual maturity represented among believers, but this should never be a source of pride. If God is the one who grants and accomplishes spiritual growth in believers, then how can they take any credit? Humility rather than pride is a fruit of maturity; an elitist attitude is actually a mark of immaturity.

Manipulation is a term that describes an unbiblical understanding of how God responds to human actions such as prayer. God's people often encountered the views of other pagan and polytheistic religions. Many of these religions believed that if a man or woman performed an appropriate action on earth, a god or gods had to respond in a particular way in heaven. For example, Canaanite religion believed that if worshipers of the god Baal offered the correct type of sacrifice, Baal would be moved (or forced) to send the rain and bountiful harvest they desired. Sometimes manipulation involved the use of incantations. Those who use incantations believe that if they repeat certain words, God must respond in a particular way. When applied to the practice of intercession with the God of the bible, manipulation is clearly wrong. Our prayers cannot force God to do something – he is not bound to respond a certain way simply because we ask. The authors of Scripture are careful to affirm God's sovereignty, that is, his freedom from our manipulative efforts.

A Final Word: Biblical Characters Really are Like Us

As we begin the *Journey into Intercession*, we must keep in mind another important idea: characters in the bible are just like us. Unfortunately, many Christians read the stories of the bible as if the characters were superhuman saints (or sinners, as the case may be). We read about Abraham and marvel at him as a man of impossible faith and righteousness. We read about Moses, Mary and Paul and assume that the intimacy of each one's relationship with God was unique, unattainable by "normal" believers like us.

The fact is that Abraham, Moses, Paul, Hannah and Mary, were all "normal" believers. Yes, God chose to use them in very special ways at very special times in history. Yet their lives were just as grey, just as difficult and convoluted as our lives. They did good things and bad, obeyed and disobeyed, had successes and failures. Scripture records their lives for us so that we can see that their experiences of God were not unique but rather characteristic of the kind of personal relationship God desires with all his people. Dallas Willard puts it this way:

> We must enter into our study of (the bible) on the assumption that the experiences recorded there are basically of the same type as ours would have been if we had been there. Those who lived through those experiences felt very much as we would have if we had been in their place. Unless this comes home to us, the things that happened to the people in the bible will remain unreal to us. We will not genuinely be able to believe the bible or find its contents to be real, because it will have no experiential substance for us.[4]

As we take the *Journey into Intercession*, we must keep this attitude in mind. God desires a relationship with you such as he had with Abraham and with Mary. Though the particulars of your story may be different, the purpose and goals are the same. God seeks glory by drawing you and others into an intimate, personal, and fulfilling relationship with himself. This relationship is what the *Journey into Intercession* is all about.

The Old Testament Journey

Day 1 – Abraham and Ishmael (Genesis 17)

In this chapter, God appears to Abraham to reaffirm the promises he has already made to Abraham and Sarah. In Genesis 12:1-3, God had promised them a special land, many descendents and blessing on them and their descendents and on other nations through them. While God is the one who will initiate and fulfill this promise, he asks Abraham and his male descendents to undergo circumcision as a sign of their participation in this agreement. He also tells Abraham that Sarah, who is now past the age of childbearing, will be the one through whom he will fulfill the promise of descendents.

Abraham's response is surprising – he laughs! How can a man 100 years old, with a wife 90 years old, bear a son? He then asks that God might simply bless Ishmael, the son Abraham had conceived with Sarah's maidservant Hagar (see Genesis 16). God immediately replies that he has heard Abraham's request and that he will bless Ishmael, making him into a great nation, though Ishmael and his descendents will not be part of the people of promise. Abraham responds to God by circumcising that very day all the males in his household, including Ishmael.

Reflection

It is remarkable that while the LORD's focus in this incident was clearly on the plans he had for Abraham's descendents through Isaac, Abraham himself is still thinking about Ishmael, and God hears and responds to Abraham's concerns. These concerns for Ishmael are not an indication of lack of faith, but of a faith that has room to grow, since it is still limited in its understanding of how God can accomplish his purposes. God graciously honors Abraham's sincere request, at the same time pushing him to a deeper understanding of the answer to the question God himself poses in Genesis 18:14, "Is anything too hard for the LORD?" Obviously, the answer is an unqualified "no."

In the same way, God meets us where we are in faith and graciously responds to our prayers, while at the same time opening us up to greater realities than we can even imagine. On the *Journey into Intercession*, he will lead us to the realization that nothing is too hard for him, and along the way increase our faith so that we can pray accordingly. The wordplay on "laugh" (the Hebrew meaning of the name of the son later born to Abraham and Sarah, i.e., Isaac) is important here. Both Abraham and Sarah (see 18:10-15) laugh at the thought of God doing what appears to them impossible. Perhaps we too laugh incredulously at the thought that God might do certain things. As God helps us to grow in our faith, we will learn to laugh instead as a joyful response to his incredible answers to our prayers.

There are two other things worth reflecting on in this passage. The first is that God has a conversational relationship with Abraham. That is, for Abraham God is not a distant deity to be feared and appeased when necessary, but a friend who lovingly dialogues with Abraham. God desires this type of relationship with all believers in Christ, and God desires to have this type of relationship with you. Second, Abraham's response to God shows a proper recognition of who God is. That response is to obey God by carrying out the act of circumcision God had prescribed. While God is Abraham's friend, he is also the Creator and Lord of all that exists. Abraham's interaction with God here shows the tension that we live with as intercessors: we are at once God's intimate friends and God's humble servants.

Exercise

A simple but important pattern for prayer is to begin by thanking God for one of his character traits, then to pray for yourself or someone else according to that trait. This passage speaks of God's ability to do what seems to us impossible, so praise him in writing that this is true of him. Then write a prayer that asks God to give you faith to believe that nothing is impossible for him. Ask him also to bring to mind a situation that seems impossibly difficult for you or someone else. When something comes to mind, write it down and ask God to demonstrate his ability to do the impossible. Thank him for hearing and responding to your prayer (as we will see, this attitude of thanksgiving is very important for intercessory prayer).

Day 2 – Abraham and Lot (Genesis 18:16-33)

Abraham is in a position to intercede again, this time for the people living in Sodom and Gomorrah. Earlier in the chapter, the LORD, represented by three men, appeared to Abraham. He now tells Abraham that in a year Sarah will have the promised son. When the men get up to leave, the LORD considers whether he should keep from Abraham what he is about to do to the cities of Sodom and Gomorrah. He also reflects on the promise he has made to Abraham, having chosen him to "keep the way of the LORD by doing what is right and just." God then proceeds to speak to Abraham of his intention to visit Sodom and Gomorrah to assess their great sin.

In response to this information, Abraham boldly challenges God based on the injustice of destroying the righteous with the wicked. We often think of the wicked as those who have committed terrible evil, and thus believe that we must be in the other category (the righteous). Biblically, however, the wicked are those who choose to live their lives apart from dependence upon God. Put another way, the wicked are those who seek to live independently of God and thus to depend upon themselves. The righteous, by contrast, are those who by faith turn to God for help. Psalm 1 presents a wonderful picture of these two ways of living, and Psalm 32 shows how God blesses sinners when they turn to him for help.

In his prayer, Abraham cries out for the righteous ones in Sodom and Gomorrah. Far be it from God, he says, to treat the wicked and the righteous alike! The negotiation that Abraham then pursues seems designed to affirm God's mercy and justice. God consistently replies that he will not destroy the righteous with the wicked, even if there are only ten righteous people in the city. God then proves his just and merciful character by saving the four righteous persons (Lot's family) out of the city before he destroys it.

Reflection

It is remarkable how intimate a relationship God has with Abraham. God is free to carry out his plans any way he wants. Yet here we see what will become a common theme in Scripture: God freely chooses to put a priority on his relationship with human beings, even to the point of inviting their involvement in his deliberations and actions. This is not a mere formality but an authentic relationship. In this passage, God takes Abraham's words seriously. He does the same for us.

Abraham's words are also instructive on the task of intercession. Abraham directs his appeal to God's character. Abraham knows that God is a protector of the righteous, because this is how God has revealed himself to Abraham in their relationship. Abraham thus appeals to this aspect of God's character, pointing out that to destroy the righteous in Sodom and Gomorrah with the wicked would be unfair to the righteous. While Abraham's concern is clearly for his nephew Lot, his approach to interceding for Lot and his family is to base his prayer on what God says about himself.

Our understanding of God's character comes from Scripture. We will learn much more of God's essential character as we continue on the *Journey into Intercession*. Scripture makes clear elsewhere the divine character trait on which Abraham bases his prayer in this passage, namely that God takes care of those who trust in him (that is, the "righteous"). Psalm 32:10 puts it this way: "Many are the woes of the wicked, but the LORD's unfailing love surrounds the man who trusts in him." Since God has revealed himself in his Word as a protector of those who trust him, we can and should learn to appeal to God confident of this truth.

One other aspect of Abraham's prayer here deserves comment. In both chapters 17 and 18, Abraham directs his intercession according to knowledge given specially to him by God. Though God does not tell Abraham how to pray, he does give Abraham information that leads him to pray. In both cases, God hears and responds to his prayer. These passages therefore reveal an important principle: we should pray according to whatever God does reveal to us, always remembering that only God understands the bigger picture.

Exercise

To become an effective intercessor, it is essential to know the God to whom we pray. As we said, on this journey we will learn much more about his character. Since we have already seen that he is one who protects those who put their trust in him, write down a prayer thanking God that he is this way. You can even simply write down the words from Psalm 32:10, telling God you praise him "because your unfailing love surrounds the one who trusts in you." Then ask him to bring to mind a person that is in need of his protection. When he does, ask that he might help this person to trust him and thereby enjoy God's protection. Keep in mind that, as with Abraham, God graciously invites you to participate in his deliberation and action! Thank him for hearing and responding to your prayer.

Day 3 – Abraham and Abimelech (Genesis 20)

In this chapter, Abraham has an opportunity to intercede for a foreign ruler. Abimelech has taken Sarah into his household, and God warns him in a dream that he will punish him because she is a married woman. God tells him to return Sarah to Abraham, who will intercede for Abimelech so that he can live. God describes Abraham as a prophet, and his prayer to God is effective, so that Abimelech's wife and slave girls' are enabled again to bear children.

Reflection

We have already seen a pattern of God speaking to Abraham, which he will again do in this narrative. Here God also speaks to a foreign ruler who is clearly not a part of the people of promise. Like Abraham in Genesis 18, Abimelech responds to God's warning in a dream by petitioning God not to punish the innocent. God responds by granting his request, provided Abimelech does indeed return Sarah to Abraham. God also draws Abraham into the healing process by telling Abimelech that he must ask Abraham to intercede for him.

Why does God require Abimelech to seek Abraham's prayer? Part of the blessing promised to Abraham and his descendents was healing not just for themselves, but also through them to other nations. Abraham, a member of God's chosen people, here carries out this role as a mediator of blessing through intercessory prayer. Those who believe in Jesus Christ now function in this same role, as mediators of the Abrahamic blessings to all nations (see Galatians 3:26-29). We like Abraham can see this blessing given to others through our prayers for them.

Could God have healed Abimelech apart from Abraham's intercession? Of course. Yet once again we see God sovereignly choosing to accomplish his purpose through human means. Abraham has the privilege and responsibility of mediating God's blessings to others through prayer. This is how God has chosen to accomplish his plan.

It is also worth noting that this whole incident revolves around the promises God had made earlier to Abraham and Sarah. Obviously, apart from Abraham, Sarah cannot fulfill the promise of a son. God thus orchestrates Abimelech's dreams and Abraham's prayers to protect the fulfillment of his greater plan, including the bringing of a Savior into the world through the descendents of Abraham and Sarah (see Matthew 1:1-17). We are not to think that it is Abraham's goodness that leads to this fulfillment. In this passage (and so many others like it), Abraham is actually putting the promise in jeopardy. Rather, it is God's faithfulness in spite of Abraham's (and our) failures that leads to the fulfillment of the promise. This is reason to be very thankful to God!

Exercise

Give thanks to God that he has made you a descendent of Abraham, and called you to mediate his blessing to others just as he did Abraham. Has anyone asked you to pray recently? Have you done so? Take time to write out exactly what this person asked you to pray for, and then ask God for insight into how you can intercede. Oftentimes there are deeper needs we may not be aware of behind requests for prayer. Abimelech could not have understood all the spiritual dynamics of the situation he had gotten into. Listen as you pray, and write down any insight the LORD gives you. As you pray, remember that it is God's will to use people such as you to carry out his ministry here on earth, so you can pray in great faith that he will make your prayers effective. Thank God for hearing and responding to your prayer.

Day 4 – The Servant of Abraham and a Wife for Isaac (Genesis 24)

In this chapter, Abraham is seeking a wife for Isaac, the child finally born to him and Sarah. Abraham gives his servant strict instructions to find a wife for Isaac among Abraham's relatives rather than among the Canaanites. If he finds a woman who will not return with him to Abraham and Isaac, then Abraham releases the servant from his obligation.

When the servant arrives at a well in Abraham's homeland, he asks the LORD to show kindness to Abraham by causing the chosen woman to respond with certain words. The Hebrew word translated kindness is *hesed*, a word that Scripture often uses to refer to God's unfailing love and that we have already seen in Psalm 32:10 (cited above). Rebekah responds to the servant appropriately, and when the servant finds out she is from Abraham's family, he worships the LORD for showing his kindness and faithfulness to Abraham. Later, Isaac must pray for Rebekah in her barrenness, an entreaty that the LORD answers (Gen 25:21b).

Reflection

Both of these prayers revolve around the fulfillment of God's promises to Abraham and his descendents. The finding of a non-Canaanite wife from Abraham's kin emphasizes God's sovereign provision in keeping his promise, since Abraham and his family were sojourners in the midst of Canaanite culture. Rebekah must be able to bear a child to have the line of promise continue. In both cases, God grants the petition.

Just as we can and should appeal to God based on his character, so also we can and should appeal to him based on his promises. These promises reflect God's purposes for us.

His purpose for Abraham and Sarah was to restore blessing to all other peoples through them and their descendents. As New Covenant believers, we are a part of this purpose as well, since by our faith in Jesus Christ we are the spiritual descendents of Abraham and Sarah. When we intercede according to God's promise to bless all people through us, we can be sure God hears and responds. This is what Jesus means when he teaches us to pray for God's kingdom to come and God's will to be done. This is simply another way of asking God to make good on the promises of restored blessing he has made to his people through the ages.

Exercise

Write down a prayer in which you thank God for making you part of the promised line of Abraham, through which he will restore blessing to all peoples. Thank him also that he has given you the privilege of mediating his blessing to others through intercessory prayer. Ask him to fulfill this purpose in you by making you an effective intercessor. Thank him for hearing and responding to your prayer.

Day 5 – Moses and Pharaoh (Exodus 8:1-15, 20-32; 9:13-35; 10:1-20)

Moses is a model intercessor. The narratives describing Moses portray him as, among other things, a mediator standing between a holy God and his rebellious people. Moses must often mediate by interceding for the people, asking God to forgive and deal mercifully with them. In this way, he points clearly to the role that Jesus Christ would play as a mediator. Like Jesus, Moses' mediation goes beyond asking for forgiveness and mercy on behalf of the people of Israel. He will also intercede for Pharaoh, and will pray for healing for individuals within Israel (e.g., Miriam) and for God's provision and presence to go with his people.

In this passage, Moses prays for Pharaoh and Egypt. On four different occasions during four different plagues, Pharaoh asks Moses to call upon the LORD to stop the plague. Scripture uses different words to describe Moses' prayers. Sometimes it labels his prayers entreating, sometimes crying out and sometimes simply spreading out his hands to the LORD. In each case, the LORD hears his intercession and stops the destruction. In two of the cases, Moses states the reason the prayer will be answered, "so that (Pharaoh) may know there is no one like the LORD our God" (Exodus 8:10), and "so (Pharaoh) may know the earth is the LORD's" (Exodus 9:29). Moses clearly roots his prayers in a concern that God make his true nature known to Pharaoh and the Egyptians. He is unique among the (so-called) gods worshiped by the Egyptians. In fact, he is the God who possesses and rules the whole world. His responses to Moses' intercessions would be a way of revealing these things about himself.

Reflection

It is always best for us that we recognize God for who he really is. It is easy to project onto God our own ideas of who he should be, with the result that we think of him in ways that are not accurate. Since God is concerned that we understand him rightly, he uses a variety of means to reveal himself to us. In this passage, the revelation of his uniqueness and sovereignty occurs in response to Moses' prayers for his intervention. His answers to these prayers in the presence of Pharaoh and the Egyptians would serve to make them aware of this God's true character and power. Contrary to what the Egyptians believe, there is no god like Israel's God, and all of creation actually belongs to him. The sooner the eyes of Pharaoh and the Egyptians are opened up to this spiritual truth, the sooner they will enjoy the benefits that come from a right view of reality, what we could call a correct "world view."

This revealing of God's true nature is what Scripture means by glorifying God. When people see who he really is, God is glorified. It is always appropriate to pray that God would reveal his glory to others. How God chooses to reveal his glory will differ from person to person and from time to time. It is a good thing to pray as Moses did that God would answer someone's request so that he or she would see God for who he really is. As we intercede for others, a concern for God's glory should drive our prayers, just as it did Moses' prayers.

Exercise

Give thanks to God that he is the one, true God, and that he is not only the creator but also the ruler of this world. Then ask him to bring to mind the name of someone who does not understand these truths. When he does, ask him to work in their life in such a way that they see his true glory. It may be that this person has a specific need such as Pharaoh had. If the LORD brings this to mind, pray that he would meet their need in a way that helps them to see who he really is. Then thank him for hearing and responding to your prayer.

Day 6 – Moses and Israel in the Wilderness (Exodus 15:24-25; 17:1-7)

After the people of Israel leave Pharaoh and crosse the Red Sea, they walk through a deserted land and begin to complain. Twice before they reach Mt. Sinai, they grumble about lack of drinking water, and Moses asks God to provide for their thirst. The LORD meets Israel's need at Marah by showing Moses a piece of wood which, when thrown into the water, makes it drinkable. At Massah and Meribah the LORD provides water for the people when Moses obediently strikes the rock with his staff.

In the first incident, we are told explicitly that the LORD was testing the Israelites to see if they would trust him enough to do what he commanded. A similar theme is given in the second incident, in which the place is called Massah (testing) and Meribah (quarreling), because "the Israelites quarreled and because they tested the LORD saying, "Is the LORD among us or not?" This question is clearly to be answered in the affirmative in light of all God had done so far (e.g., delivering Israel from Egypt through plagues and the crossing of the Red Sea) and is now doing (i.e., providing water in the wilderness).

Reflection

The focus on testing in these narratives draws our attention to the question of faith: do the Israelites trust the LORD? The people of Israel, like people in general, seem to have a very limited understanding of both God's concern for them and his power. Moses, on the other hand, is aware of the promises God has made to build and sustain a great nation from the descendents of Abraham. For this to happen they must have water to drink! Not only this, but he trusts that God is able to do the impossible. For these reasons, he is able to intercede effectively on Israel's behalf. Indeed, he must intercede, since only he seems to be aware that the God they worship desires to meet their needs in surprising ways. God really is among them, and faith in this presence leads Moses to intercede and receive answers to requests that Israel has not even thought to ask. Likewise, our role as intercessors is often to step in and pray for things that those around us might not even think to commit to prayer.

It is significant also, that God's provision comes in response to prayer. In both incidents, God could simply have provided what was necessary apart from Moses' intercession. However, the fact that the provision comes in response to Moses' request points to an important lesson. God wants us to learn to depend on him. Prayer is a way of eliciting faith from us that expresses our recognition that he is the one who meets our needs. Had God simply given the Israelites water in each case, he would have met their needs but they would not have seen that he was the one meeting them. Moses' prayer adds an element of human involvement and responsibility that keeps the focus on God's provision.

Our intercessory role follows the same pattern. Could God not help those for whom we pray apart from our prayers? Of course he could! This, however, is not what God has chosen to do. Instead, he has granted us the privilege of being involved in his actions on others' behalf. As we pray for others, we speak our faith that God is the one who can meet our needs. God delights to prove himself up to the task, because when he responds we see more clearly his glory.

Exercise

Offer thanks to God that he is a God who is able to meet our needs, even in seemingly impossible ways. Thank him also that he has given us the privilege of being partners with him through prayer to meet those needs. Ask him for the faith to trust that he is with you as a believer in Christ, just as he had promised to be with Israel in the wilderness. Ask him also to bring to mind anyone for whose needs you can pray. When he brings people to mind, pray for them and ask that they would trust God more because he has responded to your prayer on their behalf. Then thank him for hearing and responding to your prayer.

Day 7 – Moses and the Golden Calf, Part 1 (Exodus 32:1-14)

One of the most significant examples of intercession in all of Scripture occurs in Exodus 32-34. Scholars have said and written much on the complexity of these chapters. What are of concern to us are those elements that bear directly on intercessory prayer. Moses is here, once again, an intercessor, and we have more than in any previous passage a picture of how God's own character and our task of intercession go hand in hand.

Exodus 32 begins with a description of the people of Israel awaiting Moses' return from Mt. Sinai. They have recently agreed to uphold their end of the Sinai (or Old) Covenant, saying, "We will do everything the LORD has said" (Exodus 19:8). Yet Moses' delay in coming down the mountain throws them into a panic, and they ask Aaron to make a god (or gods, the language is ambiguous) that will go before them. Aaron does this, forming a golden calf, and the Israelites then say, "This is your god, O Israel, who brought you up out of Egypt" (Exodus 32:4). Ironically, Israel has immediately fallen into the very idolatry against which the ten commandments Moses is on the mountain receiving would warn them. What Israel was trying to do through the making of a golden calf idol was to secure God's presence with them in a physical form. Sadly, the chapters preceding this incident (Exodus 25-31) describe how God himself intended to provide such a physical presence for Israel in the tabernacle.

God's response to Israel's idolatry is severe since idolatry represents a breach of the covenant to which they had just agreed. Moses' intercession appeals directly to God's character. Does it make sense to destroy his own people that he had just brought out of Egypt? What will the Egyptians say about a God who brings his people into the desert only to slaughter them? What about the promise God had made to establish a great nation from Abraham's descendents and to bring them to their own land? Due to Moses' prayer, God immediately relents concerning the destruction he was going to bring on Israel.

Reflection

Much like Abraham in the book of Genesis, Moses' here bases his intercession on a close and personal relationship with God. The LORD listens and responds to Moses' pleading. In fact, God seems to invite Moses to participate in formulating a response. We have already seen a similar deliberation with Abraham in Genesis 18. God's words in Exodus 32:10, "Now leave me alone so that my anger may burn against them and that I may destroy them," emphasize the significance God places on the relationship with Moses. He expresses a reluctance to act against Moses' wishes if Moses is present. Though God told Moses to leave him alone, Moses disregards the request, and continues the dialogue. Such a bold pursuit of God in prayer is actually an act of faith, based as it is on confidence in God's promises and character. Moses is convinced that God will act reasonably, with concern for his reputation (i.e., glory) and in a manner consistent with his covenant promises to the patriarchs. God, having drawn Moses into the situation, honors this boldness by stopping the calamity. The picture of God is one that shows him putting a priority on his sovereign choice to be relationally responsive to those who enter seriously into the dialogue of prayer.

How bold are you when you pray? We often avoid boldness with God because we fear retribution for somehow defaming God. Yet Moses is utterly bold. His boldness is driven by a deep understanding of himself as chosen and loved by God, and "Perfect loves drives out fear" (1 John

4:18). Moses is thus able to express openly his concern that God might be defamed in others' eyes if God chooses to act in a particular way, and that God might risk going against his own promises. Is concern for God's reputation a driving force in your prayers? Are you secure enough with God to speak this boldly with him?

God wants you to have the same security in your relationship with him that Moses did. Such security depends not on your goodness or ability to keep God's laws, but on a deep understanding of his love for you in Jesus Christ. The New Testament describes the incredible depth of this love in passages such as Romans 8:28-39, Ephesians 3:14-19, and 1 John 4:18. Being secure in God's love for you enables you to be bold like Moses.

Exercise

Thank God that he has a love for you that is beyond comprehension. As a means of doing this, read Romans 8:28-39 and Ephesians 3:14-19, and then write down what God himself says about his love for you. Pray that he would help you not just to know about this love but also to experience it. Pray that your experience of his love would help you to be bold in intercession like Moses was. Ask God to give you a deep sense of concern for his reputation. Thank him for hearing and responding to your prayer.

Day 8 – Moses and the Golden Calf, Part 2 (Exodus 32:15-35)

Though God relented from destroying the Israelites after Moses' intercession, Moses uses the Levites to carry out a symbolic judgment of 3,000 Israelites. The next day Moses tells the people he himself will seek to atone for their sin. This atonement is important because it addresses the rift in the relationship between God and his chosen people caused by the golden calf incident. It's one thing for Israel to have been spared God's wrath. It is quite another thing for them to be forgiven and restored as God's chosen and treasured people, and it is to the latter issue that Moses now turns.

Moses' appeal this time is based on his own willingness as their leader to suffer in their place. He says to God, in essence, "If you won't forgive their sin, then punish me in their place." God responds by telling Moses he will blot out from his book whomever has sinned against him. When the time comes for him to punish, he will do just that. In verse 35, we are told that the LORD struck the people with a plague because of their sin with the golden calf, which may or may not be the fulfillment of this threat.

Reflection

In this second of three prayers related to the golden calf incident, Moses hears what appears to be a "no." God listens to his offer to be punished in place of Israel, but responds by affirming his independence to choose whom and when he will punish. Interestingly, this "no" will become a huge "yes" in the following chapters. Thus the story is not over, but is still in the making, and both Moses and Israel have a part to play in how the story turns out.

Whereas God has invited us to intercede for others as a vital means of participating in his plan, we must remember that he is still God. It is possible for us to fall into one of two errors in intercession. One is the error of complacency, mistakenly attributing to God a type of control that eliminates any purposeful participation by humans. The other is the error of arrogance, wrongly assuming that we can manipulate God into responding in certain ways if we do our part. This passage warns against the latter error by reminding us that God is not subject to our manipulations. Our view of intercessory prayer must balance an understanding of God's independence with an understanding of his choice to use our prayers to accomplish his purposes.

Exercise

Thank God that he is sovereign and free from your control. Thank him also that he has chosen to let you play a significant role through prayer in the accomplishment of his purposes. Ask him to help your prayers for others to exhibit a proper balance between expectation that he will do as you ask and submission to his sovereign will. Also, take time to look back over the prayers you have prayed so far (days 1-7). Write down any observations you notice about the way God has answered your prayers, and what you can learn from these observations. Then thank him once again for hearing and responding to your prayers.

Day 9 – Moses and the Golden Calf, Part 3 (Exodus 33-34)

God has commanded Moses to lead the people of Israel to the Promised Land. He will send an angel ahead of them, but he himself will not go because they are a "stiff-necked people," and he might destroy them on the way. Such a threat appears mean-spirited, yet it actually points out an important aspect of God's character. He is mercifully withdrawing his "tabernacling" presence (that is, his presence mediated through the tabernacle) from Israel to protect them from his wrath when they sin. Israel's covenant breaking activity has harmed their relationship with the LORD. He will keep his promise to give them the land, but will not dwell among them as he had said. The people of Israel respond to this news with mourning and the removal of the jewelry they had taken from Egypt, perhaps symbolizing they are no longer the covenant people.

Moses, whom the text describes as speaking with God as a man speaks with his friend, again appeals to God regarding Israel. He complains that God has not told him who would go with him to the land of promise, and asks God to teach him his ways. He then asks God to remember that Israel is God's people. God's response, which clarifies Moses' requests, is that he would indeed go with Moses to the Promised Land and that he would give Moses rest. Moses is unsatisfied with this, asking that God not send the people unless God's presence is not only with Moses but also with the people of Israel. This time Moses appeals to God's reputation and promise. How will they know God is pleased with Moses and Israel if God does not go with them? What will distinguish Moses and Israel from all other people if God does not go with them?

God's response is immediate and striking, "I will do the very thing you have asked, because I am pleased with you and I know you by name" (33:17). Moses then asks for a sign of the LORD's presence, saying, "Now show me your glory." God in turn speaks to Moses of his fundamental character, declaring that he is good, compassionate, gracious, slow to anger, abounding in love, faithful and forgiving. Moses' response is to fall and worship (34:8), and then to petition again based on God's self-revelation. In this request, Moses asks for what is still lacking in Israel's status due to the golden calf incident, namely, full forgiveness and restoration to full covenant status. Apart from forgiveness, Israel cannot survive in God's presence. And Moses and Israel do not want to live apart from God's presence.

Remarkably, God responds by making what we may call a "new" covenant with Israel. Unlike the covenant made at Sinai, which Israel had broken almost as soon as they agreed to it, God here makes a unilateral covenant, at his own initiative, with no conditions for Israel to fulfill. God has revealed himself as characterized by grace, and here he takes the initiative to reestablish the covenant with Israel based solely on his gracious character.

Reflection

Moses' prayer for Israel follows God's self-revelation. It is significant that whereas Moses asks to "see" God's glory, the revelation is primarily "heard." God twice pronounces his personal, covenantal name, Yahweh (typically translated as "Lord" with all capital letters, "the LORD"). He then describes his merciful character. He is gracious and compassionate, slow to anger, rich in love and faithfulness, and forgives wickedness and rebellion for thousands of generations (see Exodus 20:6). Nonetheless, lest his people take such grace for granted, he does punish sin for three or four generations.

This spoken revelation is significant for us as intercessors in that it reveals, in terms that are fit for prayer, what the glory of God consists of, that is, his grace and compassion! To pray for the revealing of God's glory is to pray for his gracious mercy to be experienced – God receives glory when we come to understand his true character. Moses petitions for this very thing in 34:9, asking that God might forgive the wickedness and sin of this stiff-necked people. Once again then, it is God's revelation of his character that forms the foundation of intercessory prayer. This revelation is the most comprehensive and hopeful yet – God is a god of grace. This theme will become primary in the rest of Scripture.

Exercise

Thank God that he has revealed his character as gracious, compassionate, slow to anger, rich in love, faithful and forgiving. Ask him to give you a deeper experience of each of these character traits. Then ask him that you might learn to pray more effectively according to his true character, as he has revealed it in Scripture. Thank him for hearing and responding to your prayer.

Day 10 – Moses and Israel (Numbers 11)

Though this chapter appears two books later than the golden calf incident, not much time has passed in the narrative. The Israelites have just set out from Mt. Sinai toward the land of promise. The people of Israel are again complaining. God's anger literally burns like fire among them, a reminder of the wrath God has already exhibited toward his rebellious people. Moses prays to the LORD and the fire ceases. Sadly, the people continue to complain, this time about God's marvelous provision of manna to eat. "It was so much better in Egypt!" The LORD's anger burns again.

Moses' response is also a complaint. Why are you doing this to me? What did I do wrong to deserve the responsibility of carrying these people? Did I conceive and give them birth? How can I feed them the meat they crave? Moses tells God the burden of these people is too heavy for him to bear, and says he would rather God put him to death than make him continue.

God's response is twofold. First, he addresses the problem of leadership by telling Moses he will spread the burden by putting his Spirit upon seventy elders. Moses gathers the seventy and they begin to prophesy by the Spirit. When two elders who were not among those gathered also begin to prophesy, Joshua asks Moses to quiet them. Moses' response is surprising: "I wish that all the LORD's people were prophets and that the LORD would put his Spirit on them!" (11:29).

God's second response is to tell the people he will give them meat to eat until they are sick of it, because they have "rejected the LORD who is among you" (11:20). Moses, showing a lack of understanding of God's ability to do the impossible, questions how God can provide such meat. God replies: "Is the LORD's arm too short?" He keeps his word by sending a wind (the Hebrew word for wind, *ruach*, is the same as the word for spirit) carrying quail for the people to eat. Even as they are eating it, the LORD's anger burns and he sends a plague among the people.

Reflection

This narrative marks a significant turning point in the history of God's people and, more specifically, in the history of intercessory prayer. Up until now, Moses has been Israel's intercessor, overseeing a flock of perhaps two million men, women and children. He has come to the end of his rope in trying to carry this responsibility. He cries out to God not only for them, but also for himself. God responds by distributing the Holy Spirit more broadly among his people.

The implications for intercession are significant. First, Moses' role as a leader, including his intercessory role, clearly depends on the presence of the Holy Spirit in him. The Spirit is the agent that enables Moses to carry out his duties. Second, God now distributes much more broadly the responsibility of interceding. One person, as godly as he might be, cannot carry the whole load. Moses himself even wishes that God would give all of his people the Spirit as he did the 70 elders. One can see clear allusions to what God would do through Christ and the New Covenant, when such broad distribution of the Spirit (and thus the ability to intercede) will be the case (see Joel 2:28-32; Acts 2:1-21).

We may also note that God's anger is still an issue. Clearly, the type of relationship God is trying to establish with Israel demands trust and faithfulness, and when Israel fails to exhibit these attitudes, God responds with jealous anger. God does not treat lightly the people's ungrateful responses to his goodness.

Exercise

The Holy Spirit is essential to the task of intercession. Thank God that he has given us his Holy Spirit so that we (believers in Christ) have become the place where God now dwells. Thank him also that this same Holy Spirit enables you to pray for others just as Moses and the seventy elders did. Ask that he would pour out his Spirit in fuller measure, as described in Acts 2:17-18, so that there are more people who can intercede effectively for others. Thank God for hearing and responding to your prayer.

Day 11 – Moses and Miriam (Numbers 12)

Here the topic of Moses' leadership is again at issue. His siblings Miriam and Aaron slander him because of his foreign wife. More importantly, they seek to equate themselves with Moses, as if his gifts and calling were not different from theirs. Scripture parenthetically describes Moses as the most humble man alive, apparently not an attribute his brother and sister share or value.

The LORD calls all three of them to the tent of meeting, where he makes it clear that his relationship with Moses is indeed unique. Why then were they slandering Moses? When the LORD's presence leaves, Miriam finds herself covered with leprosy, a result of God's anger. At Aaron's urging, Moses cries out to God to heal Miriam. The LORD's response is to require that they treat Miriam as the law specified for such a skin disease (Leviticus 13:4-6). It is fair to assume that after the specified seven days she was clean. God thereby answered Moses' prayer for her healing.

Reflection

It is a wonderful thing to see gifted leaders like Moses retain their humility. So often, when God gives us special gifts, including intimate relationship with himself, we can become prideful. Such elitism is a terrible sin, for it is in essence a taking of glory from God (to whom it rightly belongs) and giving it to oneself. This fundamental sin is what Paul addresses in Romans 1:25: "They exchanged the truth of God for a lie, and worshiped and served created things rather than the Creator – who is forever praised. Amen."

Here it is not Moses, but rather Miriam and Aaron, who battle pride. Having seen the broadening of leadership through the giving of the Spirit in Numbers 11, they seem to resent any indication that Moses is still different. Such a flattening of the landscape of spiritual maturity is just as wrong as spiritual elitism. Spiritual dumbing down, like spiritual elitism, is a danger for those who intercede for others. Both attitudes represent pride, and we must pray against them.

There is, in fact, such a thing as spiritual progress, and not all people progress with the same fervor or at the same rate. God affirms that his relationship with Moses is indeed different from that with Aaron and Miriam. Moses maintained his humility even with such a special relationship with the LORD. In the same way, we ought always to seek greater intimacy of relationship with God and greater effectiveness in prayer. At the same time, we must humbly realize that humility and intimacy with God are gifts of God, not things for which we should take prideful credit.

Exercise

Give thanks to God that he desires us to grow in intimacy of relationship with him, and in effectiveness of prayer. Ask him for these things. Also, ask him for a humble spirit such as Moses had. Ask that he might make you like Moses, both humble (12:3) and one with whom God speaks face to face (12:8). Thank him for hearing and responding to your prayer.

Day 12 – Moses and Israel (Numbers 14)

The people of Israel sent spies into the land of promise (Numbers 13), and most of the spies returned with frightening stories of the people in the land. Once again, they raise voices of complaint, accusing Moses and God of having led them out of Egypt only to slaughter them in another land. Joshua and Caleb stand against the tide, reminding the people that because the LORD is with them they have nothing to fear.

The LORD appears to Moses in the tent of meeting and expresses his intention to destroy the people because they will not trust him (14:11; see also Deuteronomy 9:23-24). Just as in the golden calf incident (Exodus 32:10), God says he will make Moses into a great nation. Once again, just as in that incident, Moses asks God to relent concerning this destruction. First, he appeals to God's reputation. He says the Egyptians and the people of Canaan will think God slaughtered his people since he was unable to bring them into the land of promise (see also Deuteronomy 9:25-29). Then, significantly, Moses appeals to God's own self-revelation in Exodus 32-34. He reminds God that he has declared himself slow to anger, abounding in love and forgiving sin and rebellion. Moses says, "In accordance with your great love (*hesed*), forgive the sin of these people, just as you have pardoned them from the time they left Egypt until now" (11:19).

God immediately acts in accord with Moses' request. At the same time, he will not allow the generation that left Egypt to enter the land. Only Joshua and Caleb, who trusted God, along with the next generation of Israelites, will enter the land.

Reflection

This passage reminds us of the importance of praying back to God his own statements about himself. The LORD has stated that Israel is his treasured possession, and yet here he seeks to destroy them. What will this do to his reputation? The LORD has stated that he is slow to anger and ready to forgive, and Moses the intercessor boldly asks God to live up to what he has said about himself. Moses thus uses God's own words to move him to respond positively.

Exercise

Thank God once again that he has revealed himself as a gracious and merciful God. Then take some time to commit to memory the key expression of God's character in Exodus 34:6-7: "The LORD, the LORD, the compassionate and gracious God, slow to anger, abounding in love and faithfulness, maintaining love to thousands, and forgiving wickedness, rebellion and sin." Ask him once again to help you experience these fundamental aspects of his character so that you can be a more effective intercessor. Thank him for hearing and responding to your prayer.

Day 13 – Moses, Aaron, and the Levites (Numbers 16)

This narrative concerns the attempts of the Levites to gain equal footing with the priests. God had given to the Levites, who were descendents of Jacob's son Levi, various responsibilities with respect to the tabernacle where God dwelt. He gave to those Levites specifically descended from Aaron the additional responsibility of serving as priests before him, and the Levites not descended from Aaron here express their displeasure with this distinction. Using the tactic of spiritual dumbing down that we have already seen in Numbers 12, they argue that there are no distinctions among God's people: "The whole community is holy, every one of them, and the LORD is with them" (16:3). The Levites thereby challenge the position and authority of Moses and Aaron.

Moses prays to God concerning this situation in a number of ways. First, he asks God not to accept the burning of incense by the Levite Korah and his 250 followers, because the Law does not authorize them to make such an offering. Second, when God threatens to destroy the entire community along with the rebellious Levites, Moses and Aaron cry out for God to limit his punishment to the ones who have actually sinned (i.e., the Levites). God accedes to this request, and has the community move away from those whom he will punish.

Sadly, but not surprisingly, the Israelites complain about the killing of Korah's rebels. The LORD again says he will destroy the whole community. This time Aaron, the priest, rather than Moses, intercedes for the people by atoning for their sin. As it says, "he stood between the living and the dead, and the plague stopped" (16:48).

Reflection

The issues of spiritual pride and jealousy are still with us. As with Miriam and Aaron, so now with the Levites, there is jealousy among God's people towards the God ordained positions of spiritual leaders. Both Moses and Aaron play intercessory roles here. Moses prays that the rebels will not be successful, that God would not allow it to appear that they indeed have a case. Both Moses and Aaron pray for God to limit his anger to those who were actually responsible, so that he will not destroy those innocently watching the events unfold. The basis of this plea is God's self-revelation as a God who is slow to anger and rich in love. At the same time, it is also true that he does not let the guilty go unpunished.

Leanne Payne has written of what she calls the "gift of battle."[5] What she means by this phrase is that some people receive the God-given ability to withstand the pressures and persecution that naturally arise in the presence of a ministry God is blessing. The apostle Paul understood this when he described the need for Christians to put on their spiritual armor in order to stand firm against the powers of darkness (Ephesians 6:10-18). In our passage, Moses and Aaron could not succeed without such a gift, as many misguided people have tried to thwart their ministry by challenging their calling and authority.

As intercessors, we must pray for the gift of battle. We must follow Paul's admonition to put on all of our spiritual armor so that we can withstand the attacks of the evil one. God has placed a priority on our relationship with him through prayer and, because of this, the evil one is sure to attack us when we pray.

Exercise

Thank God that he has provided all the spiritual armor necessary for you to fight the battles to which he has called you. Then ask him to give you each of the pieces of armor listed in Ephesians 6:1-18. Pray for them one at a time, and thank God after each prayer that he has heard and responded to your prayer.

Day 14 – Moses and Israel (Numbers 21:4-9)

As has become their custom, Israel continues to complain about life in the wilderness. Not surprisingly, God sends punishment, this time in the form of venomous snakes that bite and kill many people. The Israelites wisely repent of their grumbling, and ask Moses to pray that God would remove the snakes. Moses does so, and the LORD responds by telling Moses to make a snake and place it upon a pole. Anyone whom a snake bit could look at the image and live.

Reflection

Interestingly, the LORD answers Moses' request, but not exactly in the way Moses had expected. Why did he not simply remove the snakes? Why did Moses and the people have to go through the process of making and using an image in order for God to heal them?

John's gospel may point us to an answer. In John 3:14-16, Jesus says, "Just as Moses lifted up the snake in the desert, so the Son of Man must be lifted up, that everyone who believes in him may have eternal life." Then come the well-known words, "For God so loved the world that he gave his one and only Son, that whoever believes in him shall not perish but have eternal life." What is central to this passage seems also to be central in Numbers 21, that is, the need for faith on the part of the people. Had God simply removed the venomous snakes from Israel's midst, the problem would have been resolved, but no opportunity for expressing faith in the midst of difficulty would have existed. By having Moses mount the snake on a pole, those who believed could express their trust tangibly by looking to the image and experiencing healing. So too those who trustingly look to Jesus can experience healing from the effects of sin. All of this reminds us of Psalm 23. Verse 5 of that beloved psalm highlights God's willingness to prepare a feast for us in the midst of our enemies. As in Numbers 21 and John 3, faith is the key to partaking of the feast.

Christians have images such as the cross, which are powerful tools to help us develop and express our faith in God. They can also become objects of worship that replace God (see the golden calf in Exodus 32, and also what happened to the bronze snake made by Moses during King Hezekiah's time (2 Kings 18:1-4)). As an intercessor, God may want you, like Moses, to point someone you are praying for to a powerful symbol such as the cross, which helps them express their faith. For example, guiding those for whom we pray to "see" their sin and guilt nailed to the cross with Christ can be a great step toward healing. Many Christians through history have found such a use of their imagination to be greatly helpful in their walk with God. The imagination, in this sense, is not fantasy. It is seeing what is known to be real according to God's revealed truth (his Word), but unseen by the natural eye. This is what Paul refers to as seeing with the "eyes of the heart" (Ephesians 1:18). Just as God uses words to speak to our minds, he uses the symbol of the cross to speak to our hearts.

Exercise

Thank God that he provides healing from the effects of sin. Thank him also that he desires and gives us opportunities to express our faith in his healing power. Thank him that he sometimes helps us to express our faith through symbols or images such as the cross. Ask him to help you better understand how the symbols of the cross can function as a means of eliciting faith. Write down any incidents in which God used a visual image or a symbol to help you in your faith. Also ask him to help you as an intercessor to be more aware of how to help those you pray for (especially in person) find encouragement and help in symbols and images. Thank him for hearing and responding to your prayer.

Day 15 – Moses and Joshua (Numbers 27:12-23)

Moses is nearing the end of his life, and the LORD graciously shows him from a distance the land of promise, a land Moses cannot enter (see Numbers 20:1-13). Moses, the great shepherd of Israel, asks God to appoint someone to take his place so that God's people will not be like sheep without a shepherd. God directs Moses to Joshua, a man in whom is God's Spirit, and Moses is to lay hands on him and commission him in front of the entire community.

Reflection

This is a brief but important narrative. It is noteworthy that God does not appoint someone to replace Moses until Moses asks. We see here both the visionary servant leadership of Moses, and the way in which God is responsive to that leadership. Moses' faithful initiative results in God's choice of a leader for Israel. The book of Joshua will show the wisdom of this choice.

Praying for God to continue blessing lines of leadership is an important task of intercession. The church needs more than one capable leader, and anyone who acts as if he or she can carry all the weight of leadership for God's people is mistaken. Ultimately, God wants us to put our trust in him as our leader. Human leaders are simply carrying out the task of leadership on behalf of the one true Leader.

Exercise

Thank God for each of the Christian leaders he has placed in your life. Then pray for each of those leaders that they might have a right understanding of their calling, and a heart that is humble like the heart of Moses. Pray also that they would graciously allow God to raise up, in his good time, others to carry on the ministry they have begun. Thank God for hearing and responding to your prayer.

Day 16 – Samuel and Elkanah (1 Samuel 2:18-26)

I n this passage, we see intercessory prayer in a different form. God has answered Hannah's prayer for a child, and she has dedicated her son Samuel to the LORD's service as she had promised. When she and her husband visit the temple each year, Eli the priest blesses them, saying, "May the LORD give you children by this woman to take the place of the one she prayed for and gave to the LORD" (2:20). Such a blessing is a form of intercession and, as the passage says, the LORD graciously heard and responded by giving the couple three sons and two daughters.

The blessing on Samuel and his family is in contrast to Eli and his family. Eli's sons are rebellious and wicked (see 2:12-17). Eli rebukes them, and raises the question of intercession: Who will intercede for a man before God? Apparently it is one thing to sin against men, but it is another to sin (as priests) against God.

Reflection

Blessing others is a simple yet powerful way of interceding. Rather than being mere ritual, when spoken in faith a blessing can be a significant means of calling on God's presence for another person. Simple phrases like "the Lord be with you," or "the peace of the Lord go with you," can be used to bless others. Such phrases can bring change in others because we speak them in faith. Though such speech may seem awkward at first, it can be a very effective way to intercede for others.

Eli's questions in this narrative are ironic, since as priests he and his sons were supposed to be intercessors for the nation of Israel. His questions also point to the need for intercessors that can fulfill the need for those who mediate between God and humanity. Jesus Christ, of course, is the ultimate mediator. Hebrews 4:14-5:10, for example, describes him as our great high priest who sympathizes with our weakness and provides help from God in our time of need. Elsewhere his intercessory role in emphasized (Romans 8:34; Hebrews 7:25). Under the New Covenant, Jesus has now called his church to fill the role of priests who mediate God's blessings to the world. This priestly role is what reformers such as John Calvin and Martin Luther called the "priesthood of all believers."

The point is not that we are all to put on robes and begin performing marriages. What our priesthood means is that our calling as Christians includes a call to carry out Jesus' ministry in his absence. He stands between us and God, bringing God's truth and salvation to us, and bringing our needs and requests to God. In the same way, we now stand as the body of Christ between God and a sin-darkened world. Like Jesus, we are to bring God's truth and salvation to this world, and to bring the needs and requests of those in the world to God. We accomplish the latter task in part through our intercessory prayers. On the broader concept of the priesthood of believers, see for example Paul's description of his own ministry as "the priestly duty of proclaiming the gospel of God" (Romans 15:15-16). See also Exodus 19:3-6 with regard to the nation of Israel's priestly calling, and 1 Peter 2:4-5, 9-10 and Revelation 5:9-10 and 20:6 with regard to the church's priestly calling. See Hebrews 7:23-28 on the connection of intercessory prayer with the priestly calling of Jesus.

Exercise

Thank God that he has under the New Covenant called all believers to serve as mediators between God and others. Thank him that he has given us his Holy Spirit to help us carry out this task. Write down some situations in which you might carry out your priestly role by saying a blessing on someone like Samuel did with Hannah. Ask God to give you courage and faith to begin doing so, even replacing more common social greetings with ones that have spiritual significance. For example, one can easily replace "see you later" with "God bless you." When one speaks the latter with an attitude of faithful intercession, it can have a significant impact on another person's life. Thank God for hearing and responding to your prayer.

Day 17- Samuel and Israel (1 Samuel 12:6-25)

Israel has sinned by asking God for a human king to replace their true King, the LORD. Samuel here rehearses all that the LORD has done for Israel through its history. He then calls upon the LORD to send thunder and rain to demonstrate his power. This God does, and the people realize the great mistake they have made in rejecting him as their King. They ask Samuel to intercede for them so they will not die before this mighty God. Samuel encourages them to repent and follow the LORD, reminding them that the LORD has bound himself to his people and will not defame himself by rejecting them. Then Samuel says that it would be "sin to the LORD" for him not to intercede for them.

Reflection

When we realize that Scripture describes failure to intercede as sin, we begin to see that intercession is an act of obedience. Samuel, as a priest and prophet, had the role within Israel of mediating between the people and God. To fail to do so would be a breach of his calling. In the same way God calls us, as priests in the New Covenant, to mediate between God and others, including those who do not know God. As we have already seen, intercession for others is one key means by which we can mediate God's blessings. When we intercede, we stand between them and God, bringing their needs and concerns to the Lord for him to address. Therefore, to fail to pray for others is a breach of our calling as believers.

Exercise

Thank God that Jesus is our great and perfect high priest. Thank him also that he has given you and all believers the privilege of following in Jesus' footsteps by mediating between God and others. Ask him to make your church or fellowship an effective mediator, especially to those who do not believe in Christ. Ask him to let your church's words and actions speak in such a way as to draw others to God. Ask also that he might make your church a people of intercessory prayer. Thank him for hearing and responding to your prayer.

Day 18 – David and His Son (2 Samuel 12)

King David here intercedes for his ill son. As Nathan the prophet reports, this illness is a result of David's sin in the previous chapter, including the stealing of Uriah's wife Bathsheba and the murder of Uriah. David seeks the LORD on behalf of the child and for seven days fasts and lies on the ground at night. Finally the child dies, and when David learns of the death, he cleans himself up, begins to eat again and worships the LORD. When asked by his servants why he is not acting like a mourner, he explains that because the LORD might be gracious to him and let the child live, he sought the LORD while the child was alive. Now that the LORD's answer is clear, he will go on with his life as normal. Then David and Bathsheba conceive another son, whom we are told three times is loved by the LORD (his name is Jedidi-(y)ah; the last syllable is a shortened form of *Yah*-weh, as we see also in words like hallelu-*yah*).

Reflection

David's actions are remarkable because of the depth of understanding and faith they demonstrate. Though David had sinned grievously, he realizes that God's response to his prayers is not a function of his righteousness, but rather of God's merciful character. David appeals fervently to God for seven days, asking God to show mercy to his son. When God says "no," David trusts God's decision and proceeds to worship. As time goes on and God grants another son to David and Bathsheba, a son God loves, it is clear that God has answered David's prayers in an unexpected way. Though the son for whom he prayed dies, God provides another son to replace the deceased child. God thereby does show great favor to David.

We cannot state strongly enough that our success in prayer is not a function of our goodness, but of God's. All we can bring to God is our faith and an honest recognition of our sin. Like David, we must come to God and petition according to his grace and compassion, his unfailing love and faithfulness. Like David we must faithfully accept God's answers to our fervent prayers, continuing to worship him as he reveals in his time what he is doing.

Exercise

Thank God that he is gracious and compassionate, slow to anger, rich in love, faithful and forgiving. Ask him to give you confidence in these character traits rather than in your own righteousness. Ask him to reveal to you now any ways in which you think your actions have earned or made you deserve answers to your prayers. Write down and confess what the Lord brings to your mind. Thank him for forgiving you, and ask him to make you a person whose dependence is totally on Jesus' righteousness and not your own. Thank God also for hearing and responding to your prayer.

Day 19 – David and the Plague (2 Samuel 24; 1 Chronicles 21)

In these narratives, David responds to an attack by foreign enemies by taking a census. During Israel's history in the Promised Land, God's regularly shows his displeasure and judgment by sending invading forces to punish Israel. David knew this, and should have inquired of the LORD as to what was wrong. Instead, he depends on human means to meet the threat, and for this sin, God gives him three choices of punishment. David chooses the punishment that will put him most at God's mercy instead of the mercy of men, because "the LORD's mercy is great" (2 Samuel 24:14). The LORD then sends a plague on Israel, carried out by an angel. David is able to see the angel, and asks God to remove the punishment the angel brings from the people, who have not sinned. Instead, David says, "let your hand fall upon me and my family." The 1 Chronicles passage adds that the elders of Israel were with David, and that they clothed themselves in sackcloth and fell face down.

The LORD answers David's prayer by sending Gad, David's prophet, who tells David to build an altar on Araunah the Jebusite's threshing floor. David obeys this word, paying full price for the site, and building an altar on which he offers burnt and fellowship offerings. As a result, "the LORD answered prayer in behalf of the land, and the plague on Israel was stopped" (2 Samuel 24:25).

Reflection

This passage provides a wonderful example of how God not only hears our prayers but also directs them to a better and more appropriate end. David compassionately asks God to punish him and his family rather than the people of Israel. God's response is to direct David to an act of worship, namely the building of an altar and offering of burnt and fellowship offerings. When David trusts God and acts in accord with the word of the prophet, God stops the plague. Thus instead of transferring Israel's punishment to David, God transfers it onto a series of sacrifices, using David to mediate.

The way God uses David to mediate in this passage sheds great light on the task of intercessory prayer. As believers in Jesus Christ we know there is only one, Jesus himself, who can bear God's righteous judgment on our behalf. It can be tempting but dangerous for intercessors to attempt to take another person's sin or suffering upon themselves. This practice, known as substitution, may be rooted in a prideful confidence in oneself rather than Christ. As God illustrates through David, intercessors should direct such sin and suffering to the sacrifice God provides, namely, Jesus Christ. Only Christ is truly capable of carrying such responsibility. Our role as intercessors is to pray that others would cast their problems onto the cross of Christ, the only place we find true healing and help. Only in this way, can we both "bear with" (Romans 15:1-2) and help carry the weaknesses of others (Galatians 6:1-5).

Exercise

Thank God that he has given us every spiritual blessing in Jesus Christ (Ephesians 1:3). Thank him also that we do not have to bear the punishment for our own or others' sin, because Jesus has taken that punishment upon himself. Confess any ways in which you have practiced substitution, wrongly attempting to carry or bear another person's sin. Then ask God to teach you to pray for others with full confidence in Jesus' sufficiency to heal them from sin and related suffering. Ask him to bring to mind anyone who needs to know Jesus' healing and restoring power. Write down the names of these persons, and then pray that they would be willing to give their sin and suffering to Jesus so that he can carry them. Thank God for hearing and responding to your prayer.

Day 20 – David and the Preparations for Building the Temple (1 Chronicles 29:10-22)

D avid's son Solomon will ultimately build the temple for the LORD, but David anticipates that project by having the people of Israel donate out of their own wealth. David himself also gives massive amounts to this cause. After the leaders of the people give generously, the people rejoice in this wholehearted generosity, as does David. Then David prays in front of the all the people who have gathered for worship. In the first eight verses of his prayer (29:10-17), he extols God for his greatness, power and sovereignty. He exalts and gives thanks to him, acknowledging him as the source and possessor of all wealth, honor and strength. David then also confesses appropriate humility and dependence upon God for all that he and Israel have, and intercedes for the people and Solomon. He asks that God would keep the people's hearts generous and keep Solomon's heart devoted to God.

Following the prayer, David exhorts also those gathered to "praise the LORD your God." This they do, praising "the LORD, the God of their fathers; they bowed low and fell prostrate before the LORD and the king." The next day, the worship service continues with the offering of sacrifices and various offerings, accompanied by great joy.

Reflection

David's prayers are models for us in the way they combine praise and petition. In this case, David's praise centers on the generous response of the Israelites. He acknowledges that God is the one who has given them this wealth, and thanks God that the people have shown their faith in this fact by giving of their possessions. He then asks God to keep this faith alive in the people and in Solomon, and leads the people in more worship.

Worship and intercession go together naturally. To intercede, one must know God's character, and worship is simply our response to God's actions which reveal his true character. Praise should be a regular part of what we say when we pray to God.

Exercise

Write a prayer like David's in which you praise God for what he's done in your church, then petition him to do even greater things. An easy and helpful way to begin is simply to write down the words with which David praised God in 1 Chronicles 29:10-13. Then try to get more specific by thanking him for growth you've seen in members of your church. For example, David was excited that the people had responded so generously to his call for offerings. Is there something similar for which you can give thanks to God? After thanking him, pray for the people in your church that they might illustrate David's words to God: "keep this desire in the hearts of your people forever, and keep their hearts loyal to you." Thank him for hearing and responding to your prayer.

Day 21 – Solomon and the Temple (1 Kings 8:22-63; 2 Chronicles 6:12-7:6)

Solomon's prayer of dedication for the temple contains a litany of requests for other people. For Israel he asks that God would hear their prayers and forgive their sin when they pray toward the temple, which represents the dwelling place of God. Solomon bases his plea on God's character and promises. Israel is God's own people whom he brought out from Egypt (1 Kings 8:51), and God is the one who singled them out as his inheritance (1 Kings 8:53). Solomon also prays for those not among God's chosen people, asking that God would hear their prayers as well, so that they might know he is the true God.

Solomon's prayer and the exhortation following it are full of praise to God. He affirms, for example, that God is unique as a God who keeps a covenant of love with his people, that he is infinite and cannot be contained by a temple and that he alone knows the hearts of all men. He and the Israelites affirm God's faithfulness to his promises, and give thanks to him saying, "He is good; his love endures forever" (2 Chronicles 7:3). They also offer sacrifices to the LORD as an act of worship.

Reflection

In addition to its length and comprehensiveness, this prayer is noteworthy for showing us again how intercession and corporate worship function together. Within Solomon's prayer are many words of praise and thanksgiving. The broader context is also one of worship, both before and after Solomon's prayer. David's prayer in 1 Chronicles 29 shows a similar pattern.

Why are praise and thanksgiving so important to intercessory prayer? One reason is that when we praise and give thanks to God we are recognizing who he is and what he's done for us. We praise him for his character and his promises, and recognize that he is unique and incomparable. We thank him that he keeps his promises, that is, that he is faithful to who he says he is and what he says he'll do. Such praise and thanksgiving demonstrate our faith in the God to whom we pray. It doesn't make a lot of sense to pray for him to show his mercy in a particular situation, for example, unless we're willing to praise and thank him that he has both declared and demonstrated his mercy.

But praise and thanksgiving play another important role for us. Words of praise and thanksgiving provide a way for us to express our love for God. Such expressions are a vital part of any significant relationship. The book of Psalms is full of such expressions on the part of David and others. Psalm 103 is a wonderful example. Words of praise and thanksgiving naturally flow out of hearts that are, as David put it, "loyal to the LORD." Effective intercession depends on our hearts being devoted to God, as were Abraham's, Moses', Hannah's, David's, etc.

It is not too much to say that intercession is incomplete apart from praise. It is important then to make praise and thanksgiving a part of your intercessory prayer life. The prescribed exercises have consistently asked you to thank God both before and after you pray. One way to further develop this habit is by learning to pray the psalms, which regularly appeal to God while praising him for his character.

Exercise

Read Psalm 103, and then write down the things for which the psalmist praises God. For example, in 103:2-5, David praises the LORD for all his "benefits." David then lists some of these, including forgiveness of all his sins, healing of all his diseases, the redeeming of his life, etc. After you've written these down, ask God to show you how such praise and thanksgiving can help you to be a more effective intercessor. Ask him also to help you to understand what it means to love him, not simply through acts of obedience (which are essential) but also through expressions of praise and thanksgiving. Write down anything that he brings to your mind. Thank him for hearing and responding to your prayer.

Day 22 – Elijah and the Widow's Son (1 Kings 17:7-24)

During a time of famine in Israel, the LORD commanded Elijah to seek sustenance through a widow in Zarephath. Though food was scarce, the LORD miraculously provided for Elijah, the widow and her family. Sometime later, the woman's son became ill and died. She complained to Elijah, who carried the child to the room in which Elijah was staying and laid him on his bed. Elijah then cried out to God, questioning why God had brought tragedy on the woman with whom Elijah was staying. After stretching himself out on the boy three times, Elijah cried again for the LORD to restore the boy's life. The author tells us that the LORD heard his cry, and Elijah presented the boy to his mother alive.

Reflection

Three things are striking about this narrative. First, Elijah asks for something that seems quite impossible, since the boy has already lost his life. Yet the LORD, through Elijah's prayer, restores the boy to life. Second, Elijah prays with great honesty and fervor, even questioning God's action in "bringing tragedy" upon the widow. As we've seen many times already, such honesty can flourish only in a relationship built on trust and confidence in another's love. Elijah understood God's deep love and acceptance for him, and was therefore unafraid to be quite bold and even to challenge God. Third, Elijah accompanies his prayer with physical touch. Such contact between the one praying and the one receiving prayer, seen for example in the laying on of hands, is common in Scripture. Jesus often touched those to whom he ministered. Elijah's radical approach of lying on the child three times may correspond to the seriousness of the need.

Physical connection with those for whom we pray can be a powerful way of communicating acceptance and healing. When a person is hurting or grieving, physical touch such as a hand on the shoulder can express warmth and compassion. Laying hands on someone being commissioned or blessed creates a sense of connectedness to the ones praying and to the larger body of Christ. Coupled with prayers of faith, such touch can play an important role in the process of restoration and strengthening that God brings about through intercession.

Exercise

Thank God that he is able to do what seems impossible to us, such as the healing of the widow's son. Thank him also that he responds to our honest and heartfelt questioning of his purposes, just as he did with Elijah. Ask him to give you the faith of Elijah, faith to trust him to do the impossible and confident trust in his abiding love for you. Ask him to reveal to you how you can use physical touch to pray more effectively for others. Ask him also for the faith to trust him in moving beyond your comfort zone in the area of physical touch. Thank him for hearing and responding to your prayer.

Day 23 – Elijah and the Prophets of Baal (1 Kings 18:16-40)

As a prophet in Israel, it is Elijah's job to speak God's word to those who are misled. In this case, the people are worshiping both the LORD (Yahweh) and Baal, and Elijah challenges them to choose one or the other. A test is set up to determine which god is the true God. Baal fails to show up, and Elijah cries out to the LORD, asking him to reveal to those present that he is the true God, and that he is turning their hearts back to himself. The LORD sends fire that consumes not only the sacrifice Elijah prepared, but also the altar and everything associated with it. Immediately the people fall and profess Israel's God, the LORD, as the true God.

Reflection

Elijah's prayer and actions are significant because they point to a fundamental problem for many people. That problem is a distorted view of God. The people of Elijah's time thought God was one among many and, like the other gods about which they had heard, subject to human manipulation. They believed that if humans did the right things (such as offering sacrifices, speaking incantations, etc.) then God was bound to respond in a particular way. Elijah knows that the people cannot love God unless they understand his true nature. Thus his prayer is directed toward the end that the people would see the truth about God.

Many of us, as well as many of those for whom we pray, also need to adjust our understanding of God. In the church today there is much confused teaching. In addition, books, movies, television and other cultural factors have muddied considerably people's understanding of God's true nature. It is therefore a good motivation to pray that someone's eyes can be opened through answered prayer to the truth of who God really is.

Exercise

Thank God that he is consistent in his character, and that he delights to reveal his true nature in response to our prayer as he did for Elijah. Ask God to reveal more of his true character to you and others for whom you pray. Ask him also to show you if there are any ways in which your view of God needs correction. Write down anything that comes to mind, and pray that the process of coming to a truer understanding of God would continue. Ask him also to use your prayers for others to reveal his true nature to those for whom you pray, just as he did with Elijah's prayer. Thank him for hearing and responding to your prayer.

Day 24 – Elisha and the Shunammite Woman's Son (2 Kings 4:8-37)

E lisha, like his mentor Elijah, is a prophet whom God has gifted with mighty spiritual powers. As a way of thanking the Shunammite woman for providing him a place to live, the LORD enables her to bear a son. Some years later, the child tragically dies, and the woman lays his lifeless body on Elisha's bed and sets out to find him. When Elisha sees her coming, he is concerned that something is wrong, but notes to his servant Gehazi that "the LORD has hidden it (her distress) from me and has not told me why" (4:27).

The woman tells Elisha of her son's death, and he asks Gehazi to run quickly and lay Elisha's staff on the boy's face. The woman says she will not leave without Elisha, so he consents to go as well. Gehazi arrives and does as his master said, but nothing happens. When Elisha arrives, he enters the room in which the boy's body rests, closes the door, and prays to God. He then stretches his body across the boy, and the dead child's body begins to warm up. After pacing for some time, Elisha again stretches his body across the boy, and the boy wakes up. When the woman sees her boy alive, she bows down to the ground (the word translated "bow down" is commonly used of bowing down in worship).

Reflection

This narrative is noteworthy in a number of ways. First, God does not make known to Elisha the woman's need, something which seems to surprise him. The focus of the narrative is therefore on the woman's tenacious faith in Elisha's ability to heal. In this way, she is like many of the characters in the gospels, who seek Jesus with persistent and admirable confidence (for example, the Canaanite woman in

Matthew 15:21-28). Intercessors need to mirror such persistence, which God clearly rewards as an indication of faith. Elisha is like Christ in this sense, in that he mediates God's healing power to those who respond to him in faith.

Second, as we saw also with Elijah and the widow's son (1 Kings 17), Elisha's intercession is coupled with physical touch. Like Elijah, he lays his body across the body of the one who needs healing from death. The reason for this is not stated, but is does appear to be an integral part of the intercessory work Elisha performs. In any case, Elisha is obedient and his prayer is answered.

Third, the woman's response, though not explained, was quite likely one of worship. The connection between intercession and worship will become more and more obvious, and here we see that the natural response to God's mighty work of healing is to praise him.

Exercise

Thank God that he is able to do what seems impossible to us. Thank him also for giving us this woman as an example of persistence and tenacity in faith. Ask him to give you similar faith, characterized by persistence and tenacity. Ask him to reveal to you any of your prayers for others in which you have grown weary or weak. Write down what he brings to mind, and ask him to give you greater perseverance in praying for these people. This would be a good time to glance back over the prayers you've been praying on the journey into intercession, and to write down how God has answered your requests. Following the example of the Shunammite woman, express your praise and thanksgiving to God for hearing and responding to these prayers, and express your confidence that he will continue to hear and respond even in situations that seem at times hopeless.

Day 25 – Elisha and the Host of Heaven (2 Kings 6:8-23)

Elisha's role as a prophet sent by God is in the foreground here. Israel's king is wisely making use of Elisha's gift, continually asking for and receiving from Elisha divine insight into his enemy's plans. Elisha's servant becomes fearful when the enemy attempts to take Elisha away, and Elisha prays that God would "open his eyes that he may see" the host of heaven arrayed around Elisha. He also prays that God would blind the enemy army, which he does, and then Elisha leads them away to Samaria. Once they've arrived, he prays successfully that God would open their eyes so they can see where they now are.

Reflection

What a powerful reminder this is that the battle we fight is a spiritual one. The gift of spiritual sight that Elisha had, and which he prays for his servant to experience, reminds us why intercession is so vital. Intercessory prayer is a key means God has provided for us to enter onto the playing field of spiritual battle. Our faithful prayers for others work at this unseen level, so that we walk by faith not sight. Awareness of the spiritual realm, and particularly of God's victory and authority over evil in this realm, leads us to pray and act in ways that may not always make sense to others. For example, it is difficult to understand why we would forgive those who harm us, unless we comprehend the presence of a greater spiritual reality in which such forgiveness destroys bitterness and resentment, and in which God is the one who carries out justice. Likewise, to live as servants to others makes no sense apart from a greater spiritual reality in which the last are first and the first last, and in which God revealed himself in Jesus Christ as a servant.

Our prayers for others accomplish great things in this invisible but very real realm.

Exercise

Thank God that he exists and works in a spiritual realm that is real and significant. Thank him also that what goes on in this realm does impact us and those for whom we pray. Ask him to give you greater faith and awareness of this spiritual realm. Ask for greater spiritual insight and discernment so that you can pray for others as Elisha did. Thank him for hearing and responding to your prayer.

Day 26 – Kings Jehoahaz and Hezekiah, and Israel (2 Kings 13:1-6; 19:9-20, 35-37)

These two narratives share the theme of an Israelite king interceding for his subjects. In both cases the people are being oppressed by a foreign nation, due to their rebellion against the true God. Hezekiah's story is told in much more detail (in addition to this account, see also 2 Chronicles 32 and Isaiah 37). The text introduces him as a king who trusted the LORD (see 2 Kings 18:5-8). During his reign, the mighty Assyrians, who had already destroyed the northern kingdom of Israel, laid siege to Jerusalem. The author clearly states the reason for this: Israel had broken their covenant with God (18:12). The Assyrians taunt those inside the walls of Jerusalem, bragging that the LORD is no different from any of the other gods of the nations the Assyrians have destroyed. They invite those inside to submit to the king of Assyria and find protection under his wings. Hezekiah wisely seeks the prophet Isaiah's guidance on how to respond, and Isaiah assures Hezekiah the Assyrians will not be victorious.

After a reprieve, the Assyrian king Sennacherib sends a letter to Hezekiah that defames Hezekiah's God. Hezekiah seeks the LORD in his temple, lays the letter out before the LORD and prays. His prayer is short but full of depth. It includes praise, a request for God to respond and an honest recognition of how things "look." He calls upon God, asking him to prove his sovereignty to the nations by delivering his people. God speaks his intention to answer through the prophet Isaiah (19:20-34), and then carries out a massive rout of the Assyrian army. The author also describes the related death of Assyria's king Sennacherib.

Unlike Hezekiah, Jehoahaz is a king who generally disregards the LORD. Nonetheless, he does seek the

LORD's favor to release his people from oppression at the hands of the Aramaens. The author tells us that, "the LORD listened to him, for he saw how severely the king of Aram was oppressing Israel." God provides a deliverer who frees them, but the Israelites continue to worship gods other than the LORD.

Reflection

Both Jehoahaz and Hezekiah are in dire situations, having come to the end of their own resources. Both cry out for mercy, and God hears and responds. As kings over a theocratic nation (that is, a nation in which God is king), they played a special role in mediating the LORD's rule to his people. To pray for help is to recognize their personal and national dependence upon God. In both cases, the deliverance is connected directly to the king's willingness to ask for help. Thus these narratives serve as another example of how human prayer and God's action go hand in hand.

Hezekiah's prayer is a great example of an intercessory plea. He proclaims that God is the creator and ruler of all nations. He calls boldly for God to hear, see and listen to Sennacherib's blasphemous words, and for God to protect his own reputation by delivering his people. And Hezekiah honestly expresses what the Assyrian's destruction of other nations appears to reveal about the power of Israel's God.

Exercise

Write a prayer like Hezekiah's. Your prayer should follow these steps:

1. Give praise to God. Praise him, for example for his sovereignty and his willingness to answer those who call out for his mercy.

2.   Describe to him the way things appear in a difficult situation for which you've been praying. Perhaps it appears that God does not care or is not willing to intervene.

3.   Call boldly on him, asking him to answer so that his true character will be made known. Remember that your faith is in his willingness to hear and respond, not in a particular outcome.

4.   Close your prayer by thanking God for hearing and responding to your prayer.

Day 27 – Hezekiah and the Restoration of Temple Worship (2 Chronicles 29:1-31:1)

King Hezekiah began his reign by reestablishing corporate worship in the temple Solomon had built. The kings preceding him had let the temple fall into disarray, and Hezekiah obediently asked the Levites and priests to restore the temple furnishings and practices according to the Law of Moses. The people of Israel thus began worshiping together again, as the author makes clear in 29:27-30.

One of Israel's worship festivals was the Passover, given by God as celebrative reminder of how he had set them free from slavery in Egypt. Hezekiah invited all Israel, scattered as they were, to celebrate this festival. He exhorted them to return to the LORD, "For the LORD your God is gracious and compassionate. He will not turn his face from you if you return to him" (30:9). Though many in Israel scorned the invitation, others attended, so that a great crowd was gathered for worship.

In the midst of the Passover celebration, two opportunities for intercession arose. First, many of the people had not purified themselves for the festival as stipulated in the Law of Moses (see Exodus 12:43-49; Numbers 9:4-14). Therefore, according to the Law, they were not to partake of the celebration. Hezekiah prayed for them, asking the LORD to pardon those who joined in the festival even though they were not ritually prepared. The author tells us that "the LORD heard Hezekiah and healed the people" (30:20).

The second opportunity is described at the end of the account of the Passover celebration. The priests and Levites stood to bless the people present, and God heard them, "for their prayer reached heaven, his holy dwelling place" (30:27). The narrative ends with a description of the people's response to the celebration. They obediently removed and destroyed all the idols that were competing with the true God for their affection.

Reflection

The two examples of intercession in this passage show how responsive God is to the earnest appeals of his servants. Hezekiah, like Jesus, recognizes that the heart attitude is more important to God than strict adherence to ritual law (see, for example, Matthew 15:1-28). With this understanding, he appeals to God's mercy and God responds, so that the people are allowed to worship safely.

Hezekiah's understanding of God should be ours as well. Our role as intercessors is not to police God's people. Instead it is to pray for and rejoice in heart-felt response to God. Hezekiah had faith and confidence in God's mercy, which led him to intercede rather than trying to fix the situation himself. He also had the good sense to realize that the ritual rules God had given are means to the end of worship, rather than ends in themselves. And God's gracious response shows us the wisdom of Hezekiah's leadership.

God also responds to the prayer of the priests and the Levites for the people. This section shows us that blessing and prayer are equivalent, since both words are used to describe what the priests and Levites do. As we have already seen with Eli in 1 Samuel 2, to bless a person is essentially to pray for them – the LORD will respond the same way to blessings and prayers for others offered in faith.

Exercise

Thank God that he is gracious and compassionate, slow to anger and rich in unfailing love, and that he delights to respond to the prayers of those who seek his mercy. Thank him also that he is concerned about the attitude of our hearts, more than that we perfectly keep the letter of the law. Ask that God would give you a heart like Hezekiah's, with a deep understanding of what's truly important and a heart that is responsive to him. Ask him to give you confidence in his ability to fix difficult situations through prayer, rather than through your taking things into your own hands. Thank God for hearing and responding to your prayer.

Day 28 – Ezra and the Return to Jerusalem (Ezra 8)

Ezra was a priest who led Jews (from the name *Ju*-dah, the predominant tribe in Israel) back from Babylon to Jerusalem. The Jews were in Babylon because they had repeatedly been unfaithful to the LORD. Now the exile from the Promised Land was over, and the people were returning to the land.

Ezra asked those traveling to humble themselves by fasting, so that they might seek from God protection on the journey back to Jerusalem. He could have asked the Persian king for armed protection, but knew that to do so would be hypocritical in light of what the Jews proclaimed to those around them: "The gracious hand of our God is on everyone who looks to him, but his great anger is against all who forsake him" (8:22). So Ezra and the people fasted and prayed, and God answered their prayer.

Reflection

Though this passage (8:21-23) is closer to corporate petition than intercession, it illustrates Ezra's leadership in encouraging the people to pray and fast for one another. His motivation in praying is that the LORD's reputation would be protected, a reputation that the Jews had publicly proclaimed. God responds and provides them with protection.

Praying for God's protection on others is an important part of intercession. There are physical, emotional, mental and spiritual threats that we all face. The Apostle Paul, among others, constantly prays for God's grace and peace to protect those who believe in Christ.

Exercise

Thank God that his gracious hand is upon everyone who looks to him. Thank him for any ways that he has extended his gracious hand to you in the past. Ask that he would give you strength like Ezra to depend upon God rather than other people. Pray for protection for anyone you know who is in a dangerous situation, whether physically, emotionally, mentally or spiritually. Pray also for spiritual protection for yourself and others, using once again Paul's description of spiritual armor in Ephesians 6:10-18. Thank God for hearing and responding to your prayer.

Day 29 – Nehemiah (Nehemiah 9)

L ike Ezra's prayer, this prayer is closer to a corporate petition than to intercession. Nonetheless, it does represent the prayer of spiritual leaders who are praying on behalf of the people of God. It also illustrates well the relationship between praise and prayer.

The Jews are in Jerusalem after the return from Babylon, and are celebrating the feast of booths or tabernacles. However, they are not a free and independent kingdom as they were before the exile. Having gathered together and with fasting and wearing of sackcloth and ashes, they confess their sins and those of their ancestors. Scripture is read aloud for all to hear (probably the five books of Moses), and time is spent worshiping the LORD. The Levites then exhort the people to stand and join them in the lengthy and beautiful prayer recorded in chapter 9.

The prayer begins with praise, acknowledging Israel's God as the only Lord and as the creator of all that exists. It then recounts God's relationship with the people of Israel beginning with Abraham, and lists the many ways God had been faithful and trustworthy throughout many centuries of this relationship. In spite of Israel's continual rebellion and sin, God had demonstrated his compassionate character over and over again. Though he would regularly discipline them, he would never abandon or forsake them or turn his heart from them.

The actual petition begins in 9:32. Again affirming God's greatness and love and recounting Israel's sin, the prayer asks God to consider the people's plight. Though their situation is their own fault, the people cry out to God to relieve their distress according to his historical pattern of compassion. It almost seems as if the prayer never reaches the point of asking because the people are so ashamed of their own and their ancestors' unfaithful actions. Nonetheless, the prayer does lay the people's dilemma before God, and implicitly seeks his response according to his revealed character.

Reflection

We have seen other corporate prayers such as this that incorporate praise and thanksgiving with petition. This one also has an emphasis on confession, as the people mourn their disobedience. They have nothing on which to base their request to God, other than on his goodness and mercy. These are traits that he has not only spoken of but also revealed again and again to his wayward people.

Though it is lengthy, this prayer provides a wonderful model both for individual and for corporate prayer. Our sensitivities today make it difficult even to conceive of listening to the word of God from daybreak until noon (8:3), or of praying a prayer that recounts in such detail both our sin and God's compassion. Nonetheless, as intercessors we need to take seriously the extensive recounting of God's past goodness that precedes the cry for help. We have already seen that such cries for help are based not on our goodness but on God's merciful character. To recount his faithfulness in displaying this character is an important means of expressing our confidence that he will act in accordance with his nature, even if we don't feel we deserve any help. The fact is that we never deserve help, but God is willing to give it to those who ask humbly and honestly.

Exercise

Thank God that he is a God of compassion and mercy toward those who cry out for help. Then write down each time the prayer in Nehemiah 9 describes God's beneficial action towards his people in spite of their sin. For example, 9:16-18 describe how the Israelites became disobedient and ungrateful, yet God didn't desert them because of his compassion. When you have finished listing these, take time to write down ways in which God has shown similar mercy and compassion to you even when you were disobedient or ungrateful. Thank him that he has shown himself faithful in this regard, then pray that he might do the same in any current struggles you are having with temptation and sin. Thank him for hearing and responding to your prayer.

Day 30 – Job and His Friends (Job 42:7-17)

T he lengthy book of Job concludes with an intense revelation of God to his servant Job. Job has been crying out in his suffering, having lost his children, possessions and health. He questions God as to why he is suffering, since he is God-fearing and lives in integrity. His friends taunt him, calling him arrogant for assuming that his suffering is undeserved. Obviously he must have sinned to receive this punishment! Unfortunately, Job and his friends have an incomplete view of sin and suffering, believing wrongly that all suffering is a result of sin. Little do they know that God allowed Job to be tested due to his righteousness (see Job 1-2).

Beginning in chapter 38, the LORD addresses Job, revealing to Job through many examples how his ways are beyond human comprehension. Job humbly recognizes his lack of understanding (see 40:1-6). Then the LORD tells Job's friends, with whom he is angry, to ask Job to pray for them. They have not spoken rightly of God, though Job has. God tells them he will accept Job's prayer and not deal with them according to their folly. They do what God says, Job's prayer for them is accepted and God relents from his anger.

Reflection

Job is portrayed as, among other things, a true intercessor. The LORD directs others to him so that he can pray for them. And God responds to Job's prayer. His role is one of mediating between God and other people, a role given to him by God and a role Job performs. This is what intercession is all about. Others come to us to ask us to appeal to God on their behalf. And God asks us to pray for them.

Exercise

Thank God that his ways are beyond our comprehension, and that he can see and understand mysteries that we cannot even begin to fathom. Thank him also that he uses suffering not just to punish wrongdoing but also to build into us his own character. Then ask him to make known to you anyone for whom he wants you to pray. Take time to listen and to write down any names he brings to mind. Ask him also to direct your prayers for these people, so that you can pray according to their true needs. Once again, listen and write down what he brings to mind. Thank him for hearing and responding to your prayer.

Day 31 – The Suffering Servant and the Guilty (Isaiah 52:13-53:12)

The book of Isaiah centers on God's solution for cleansing the guilt of his chosen people (the nation of Israel). Israel's guilt is not just a vague feeling that they've done something wrong. It is an objective reality (whether or not they feel it) based on their continued unfaithfulness to the God who graciously led them out of Egypt.

In this passage, Isaiah describes a Servant of God who will serve as a sacrifice to remove the guilt of the people. This Servant will suffer greatly, though he has done no wrong (just like Job). His suffering will be on behalf of the people, whose guilt and iniquity he will carry, just as an innocent ram symbolically carried the guilt of a person who in faith offered it as a sacrifice (see Leviticus 5:17-19).

The last thing said about this Servant is that he "made intercession for the transgressors" (53:12). The Hebrew word translated intercession is not the one typically used in the passages we've looked at so far. It means to intercede or interpose, so that one of the Servant's roles is to intercede (presumably with God) on behalf of the guilty people. Later in Isaiah the term is used again:

> The LORD looked and was displeased that there was no justice. He saw that there was no one, he was appalled that there was no one to *intervene*; so his own arm worked salvation for him, and his own righteousness sustained him. (Isaiah 59:15b-16; emphasis mine)

The surrounding verses describe how the guilt of God's people had separated them from God, and how God would send a redeemer and establish a new covenant with his people (see especially 59:1-3, 20-21). This redeemer is the one who will intercede for the guilty people.

Reflection

Isaiah presents a picture for us of what an intercessor does. To interpose or intercede is to step in between two parties in order to bring about reconciliation. Clearly God's people needed an intercessor, because their sin had harmed their relationship with the LORD. In the same way, others we know may need us to step in to plead to the LORD on their behalf.

Isaiah also points forward to God's provision of an ultimate intercessor, one that not only intercedes but also himself carries and removes the guilt of God's people. This is more than Moses could do (see Exodus 32), and clearly more than anyone other than Jesus Christ can do. Isaiah thus teaches an important lesson to all that intercede. Our intercession is based not upon what we can do, but upon what God's Suffering Servant, his Redeemer, Jesus Christ has already done. In his death on the cross, Jesus brought reconciliation once and for all between God and his rebellious and untrusting people. As intercessors we lead people to the cross, to see both the terrible rift brought by sin and the overcoming of that rift by the death of God's Suffering Servant. Only with such an apprehension can we pray in spirit and truth for others. And only with such an apprehension can those for whom we pray be set free from the guilt and other devastating problems associated with sin.

Exercise

Thank God that he kept his promise to send a Servant that would carry our guilt and shame for us. Thank him also that this same servant, Jesus Christ, lives now to intercede on our behalf (see Romans 8:34; Hebrews 7:25). Then take time to read through Isaiah 52:13-53:12 slowly, writing down the characteristics listed there of the Suffering Servant of God. Thank God for what he has given us through the work of the Suffering Servant (for example, for becoming a guilt offering on our behalf). Then ask him to make you effective in bringing others to Jesus, God's Suffering Servant, for the healing and help they need. Thank him for hearing and responding to your prayer.

Day 32 – Jeremiah and the People, Part 1 (Jeremiah 12:1-17)

God called the prophet Jeremiah to speak to his people Israel during a very difficult time. David had died over 300 years earlier, and Israel had repeatedly rebelled against God by seeking fulfillment in idols. God decreed through Jeremiah and others that he would exile them to the land of Babylon for a time of discipline. There they would repent, and he would purify them of their idolatry and lead them back to the land he had promised to Abraham, Isaac and Jacob.

In this prayer, Jeremiah asks God to punish the wicked, that is, those who walk without faith in the LORD. Though his name is on their lips, it is not in their hearts. Jeremiah appeals to God's justice, asking how it can be that a just and righteous God would allow the faithless to prosper while the faithful in the land suffer. God's answer is that he is going to forsake and abandon his people (12:5-13), who are like a lion roaring against him. He has repeatedly told Jeremiah not to pray for this people – he will not listen to Jeremiah, nor would he listen now even to Moses and Samuel if they interceded for Israel (see 7:16; 11:14; 14:11-12; 15:1; see also Micah 3:1-3). God's forsaking of Israel is shocking, because he has continually revealed himself as a gracious and compassionate God who keeps his covenant of love forever. However, as 12:14-17 indicate, it is only for a time. After he uproots them, he will bring them back and show them compassion. The LORD will show compassion even to the nations that have plundered Israel, if they respond positively to him.

Reflection

Jeremiah's prayer appears negative, inasmuch as he is asking for God to bring punishment on the wicked. However, in asking for this he is actually asking God to bring his revealed character (his righteousness and justice) to bear on this situation. How can a just God allow wicked people to flaunt their rebellion and enjoy prosperity? Thus Jeremiah asks the LORD to punish them in order to show that he is just, and to show that he does intervene in human affairs to carry out his justice. Fittingly, he begins his prayer with words of praise related to his petition: "You are always righteous, O LORD, when I bring a case before you" (12:1).

Prayers for God to act justly in punishing others are known technically as imprecatory prayers (or imprecation). Such prayers are especially common in the book of Psalms (see Jeremiah 18:19-23 for another example). The appropriateness of such prayers for Christians is debated today, because Christ emphasized the need to love and pray for our enemies. However, these prayers model an important concept for us. Rather than seeking personal vengeance for evil, imprecatory prayers rightly ask God to be the one who carries out justice against the wicked. Our struggle is not against "flesh and blood, but against the rulers, against the authorities, against the powers of this dark world and against the spiritual forces of evil in the heavenly realms" (Ephesians 6:12). Thus we can appropriately pray for God to exhibit his true character in crushing the spiritual forces that seek to use persons for evil. Especially important is the victory over such evil powers accomplished by Jesus in his death and resurrection. We therefore take our stand in Jesus Christ, who has been given authority by God over all creation.

It is noteworthy that God not only reveals his plans to bring justice, but also asks Jeremiah not to intercede on behalf of Israel. In the book of Exodus, the LORD had asked Moses to "leave him alone" so that he could express his righteous anger against Israel for worshiping the golden calf. Now he asks Jeremiah to "leave him alone" – he will not listen to Jeremiah's request. In both of these situations, the importance to God of the relationship with the intercessor is clear. Though Moses does intercede and Jeremiah doesn't (probably because he realized the necessity of a refining judgment on the people), the intercessory prayers of both men are treated as if they are important.

Exercise

Thank God that he is a God of justice, and that he does set things right by punishing the wicked and protecting the righteous. Thank him also that in the cross and resurrection of Jesus he won the victory for all time over the spiritual forces of evil that seek to harm us. Ask him to bring to mind any injustice or unrighteousness that exists around you. As he does, pray for God to show his justice and righteousness against the evil forces that motivate this injustice or unrighteousness. Pray in the name of Jesus Christ, the one who accomplished God's victory over these evil powers. Also, be sure to thank God that he allows you to pray in this way as part of a relationship with him, a relationship that he takes seriously and values deeply. Thank him for hearing and responding to your prayer.

Day 33 – Jeremiah and the People, Part 2 (Jeremiah 42)

The Babylonians have now come upon the people of Israel, some of whom try to escape. A group of survivors, headed to Egypt for safety, stops to ask Jeremiah the prophet to pray to the LORD to show them "where we should go and what we should do." Jeremiah agrees, and the people affirm their willingness to do whatever the LORD says. Ten days later the LORD tells Jeremiah to exhort the people of Israel to remain in the land of promise, where the LORD will bless and protect them from the Babylonians and show them compassion. If, however, they choose to disobey and go to Egypt, they will be destroyed. The end of the chapter 42 and the following chapter describe how the people chose to disobey and also accused Jeremiah of lying. Jeremiah tells them they made a "fatal mistake when you sent me to the LORD your God and said, 'Pray to the LORD our God for us.'"

Reflection

It is easy to wonder just what these people sought from Jeremiah. Did they merely want an encouraging word? Did they expect him to affirm their decision to go to Egypt? And what kind of faith did they have? Certainly not a faith that trusted God enough to do what he said.

Jeremiah is put in the odd role of acting as an intercessor for a group of people who really don't want their prayer answered. He prays, and ten days later, seemingly a long time to wait, the LORD answers by giving him a prophecy for the people. Because the prophecy does not tell them what they want to hear, they ignore it.

This incident shows the complexity of issues that surround intercession. Does the one praying trust God? Do those seeking prayer trust God? And do they trust that God can use other people to intercede on their behalf? Such trust is more than mere belief in God. These people seemed to believe that Jeremiah's God existed. But their faith did not extend to confidence in what he said, or in Jeremiah as his messenger.

It is important to realize that those who intercede are responsible for their own faith, not the faith or response of those for whom they pray. When someone asks you to pray, realize that God may use your intercession to do a work in their hearts that is different than they expect. This is what happened to those for whom Jeremiah prayed. The people revealed their lack of trust as Jeremiah interceded on their behalf.

Exercise

Thank God that he responds to our prayers offered in faith. Ask him to give you, and those for whom you pray, a deep confidence like Jeremiah's in his answers to your prayers, whether or not those answers are what you expected. Thank him for hearing and responding to this prayer.

Day 34 – Daniel and His Friends (Daniel 2:1-23)

The Jews are now in Babylon. Daniel and his three Jewish friends, Shadrach, Meshach and Abednego, have risen to prominence because of their God-given wisdom. King Nebuchadnezzar had a troubling dream, and asked his sorcerers to interpret it. But he will not tell them what the dream was! When they argue that it is unfair to keep the content of the dream from them, he issues an edict that all the wise men of Babylon, including Daniel and his friends, should be executed.

When Daniel hears this he asks the king for more time to interpret the dream. Then he urges his friends to ask God to show them mercy so that they might live. That night Daniel has a vision that reveals the mystery of the dream. Daniel immediately praises the LORD, acknowledging him as the sovereign ruler and the giver of wisdom.

Reflection

Daniel's wisdom clearly extends beyond his God-given ability to interpret dreams. He also shows wisdom in asking his fellow believers to intercede for this desperate situation. They cry out to God for mercy. This is somewhat surprising, since we expect them to focus on praying for insight into the meaning of the dream. Nonetheless, as we have seen so often, appealing to God's character is at the heart of intercession. God has revealed himself as a compassionate and gracious God, and Daniel and his friends are in great need of his merciful intervention because the king has given them a death sentence. God responds by giving Daniel the insight he needs, leading to the salvation of all of Nebuchadnezzar's wise men. When Daniel explains the dream to the king, he falls at Daniel's feet and glorifies the LORD: "Surely your God is the God of gods and the Lord of kings and a revealer of mysteries, for you were able to reveal this mystery" (2:47). What a wonderful way for God to glorify himself, by hearing and responding to the faithful prayers of his servants.

Exercise

Give thanks to God that he responds to our cries for mercy. Consider a situation in which you or someone you know is in need of God's mercy. Perhaps someone has sinned and is suffering terrible consequences. Or perhaps someone is sick and in need of healing. Whatever the situation, call out as Daniel did for God to show mercy, because he is a merciful and compassionate God. Pray also that God would be glorified in the eyes of others through his response to your prayer. Thank him for hearing and responding.

Day 35 – Daniel and Jerusalem (Daniel 9)

D aniel and the Jews are still in Babylon, and Daniel realizes that Jeremiah had prophesied that exile in Babylon would last 70 years (see Jeremiah 25:11-12). So Daniel turns to the LORD and pleads with him "in prayer and petition, in fasting, and in sackcloth and ashes." His prayer is recorded in 9:4-19. In it we see a wonderful blend of praise, confession and petition for God to intervene and restore Jerusalem according to his word. Daniel proclaims God's character as a great and awesome, covenant-of-love-keeping, righteous, merciful and forgiving God. He then asks God to turn his anger from Jerusalem in a manner consistent with God's previous righteous acts (9:16), for his own reputation (9:17-19) and according to his great mercy rather than any righteousness on the Jews' part (9:18). God responds by sending the angel Gabriel to give Daniel insight into Jerusalem's future through words and a vision.

Reflection

This passage points to a number of issues regarding intercessory prayer. First, Daniel's initiative to pray comes from reading Scripture. Daniel, exiled with the Jews in Babylon, obviously has a personal interest in when and how God might restore the Jews to Jerusalem. His reading of Scripture turns his interest into fervent prayer. Second, Daniel accompanies his prayer with physical actions such as fasting and dressing in sackcloth and ashes. These symbols are, in fact, part of his prayer, since they communicate humility and dependence upon the God to whom he prays. Third, as we've seen so often, Daniel intercedes for Jerusalem in the context of worship. He praises God, offers thanks, recounts God's saving deeds and confesses. And when he asks God to respond, he asks according to specific aspects of God's character. His prayer is a wonderful example of biblical prayer, whether petition or intercession.

Exercise

Thank God that he has always shown himself to be faithful to his promises. Then follow Daniel's approach to prayer by doing the following:

1.   Read Scripture until you come across something for which you feel led to pray.

2.   Set aside a time to pray for this thing, accompanying your prayer with physical actions such as fasting, kneeling, laying down on the floor, etc.

3.   Begin your prayer by praising God, giving him thanks for things he has done for you (including, of course, saving you through Jesus Christ) and confessing your sin. Then pray for the thing about which God led you to pray.

4.   Close by thanking God for hearing and responding to your prayer.

Day 36 – Jonah and the Sailors (Jonah 1)

Jonah is a prophet who doesn't want God's grace and mercy to be extended to non-Israelites. When asked by God to proclaim judgment on the Assyrian capital of Ninevah, he runs the other way, because he knows that God is merciful and will not destroy the Assyrians. In fact, later in the book Jonah quotes directly from God's self-revelation to Moses in Exodus 34: "You are a gracious and compassionate God, slow to anger and abounding in love, a God who relents from sending calamity" (4:2). The word translated "relent" is the same one used of God's decision not to destroy the Israelites after the golden calf incident (Exodus 32:14). Jonah says he would rather die than see God relent from judgment proclaimed against the Assyrians.

Unfortunately (or fortunately) for Jonah, the LORD is a pursuing God. The boat Jonah is fleeing on is struck by a mighty storm, and each of the sailors appeals to his own god for help. The captain finds Jonah sleeping below deck, and urges Jonah to call upon his God as well. It is not clear whether Jonah does so. The sailors find out Jonah is the cause of the storm, and become greatly afraid of his God. Reluctantly, at Jonah's own suggestion, they throw Jonah overboard. As they do, they cry out for mercy to the LORD, Jonah's God, and immediately the storm subsides. The sailors then worship the LORD through sacrifice and the making of vows, while he mercifully saves Jonah by providing a great fish to swallow him and keep him from drowning.

Reflection

Jonah's reluctance to help either the sailors or the Ninevites goes against God's character, since he is a God who wants to show mercy and compassion. God's mercy is a gift, and Jonah wrongly believes that he deserves this gift while the non-Israelite sailors and Ninevites do not. Throughout the book of Jonah, God's character is highlighted, so that Jonah's actions and attitudes are a stark contrast to those of his God.

As those who pray for others, we must ask God to develop his heart of compassion within us. Jonah's pride and prejudice held him back from effectiveness as an intercessor. God's mercy triumphed anyway, and he shows compassion to the sailors, Jonah and the Ninevites. But Jonah's unwillingness to see others through God's eyes negatively impacts his participation in God's plan.

Exercise

Thank God once again that he is a gracious and compassionate God, slow to anger and abounding in love, who relents from sending calamity. Then write out the now familiar attributes of God listed in Jonah 4:2, and ask God that they may be true of you as well. Ask him to make you gracious, compassionate, slow to anger, and so on. Thank him for hearing and responding to your prayer.

Day 37 – Praying for God's Kingdom in the Psalms (Psalms 20, 61:6-8, 72, 122)

T he book of Psalms is a rich treasury of the prayers of Israel. Most of these prayers are petition by individuals within Israel or the nation as a whole, but there are also some prayers of intercession. And both types of prayers are set firmly within the context of corporate worship, for the book of Psalms is composed of many songs and poems that Israel used in its worship.

One of the key broad themes of these prayers is the coming of God's kingdom. At times, the psalmists experience God's kingdom through his protection of individuals or the nation from enemies. At other times, they experience his kingdom through release from the bondage, guilt and shame produced by sin. At still other times, they experience God's kingdom through his presence in the spiritually dry valleys of life. All of these experiences lead the psalmists to praise and give thanks to the LORD.

At the time many of the psalms were written, the earthly, human king that ruled over God's people was a physical symbol of God's kingdom. God had promised David and his descendents a special role within God's outworking of his purposes on earth. They were to lead God's people according to God's guidance and commands, and in turn he promised them his presence, blessing and protection. Many of the psalms reflect these promises, as the Davidic kings cry out to God for help and thank him for his gracious response to their cries.

In the same way, God had chosen Jerusalem as his special dwelling place. Also called Mount Zion, Jerusalem was a physical symbol of the success of the kingdom of God. When Jerusalem was fruitful and safe, God's kingdom was flourishing. And when Jerusalem came under attack, God's very reputation and purposes were in jeopardy. Thus to pray for the safety and protection of Jerusalem was more than a prayer of national pride. It was a prayer that God's purposes and promises would prevail on earth.

Reflection

The psalms assigned for this day are prayers for the king of Israel (Psalms 20, 61 and 72) and for Jerusalem (Psalm 122). They are clearly intercessory prayers, asking God's help and blessing upon others. From the perspective of the New Covenant, God has answered these prayers remarkably by sending and exalting Jesus Christ, a descendent of David, as his eternal anointed King. His presence and blessing are no longer identified with Jerusalem the city but with his people, those who follow Christ the King. In fact, these followers are called the "new Jerusalem," as the apostle John describes in Revelation 21:2-3:

> I saw the Holy City, the new Jerusalem, coming down out of heaven from God, prepared as a bride beautifully dressed for her husband. And I heard a loud voice from the throne saying, "Now the dwelling of God is with men, and he will live with them. They will be his people, and God himself will be with them and be their God."

In light of this identification of Christians as God's dwelling place, it makes sense to read the prayers for Jerusalem in the Psalms as prayers for the Church. In the same way, prayers in the Psalms for the protection and blessing of Israel's anointed king are naturally applied today to the growth and recognition of the kingdom God brought through Jesus Christ.

We will see in the New Testament that prayer for God's people, including both local churches and the universal Church, is a vital activity for Christians. This is because the people of God, consisting of all believers in Jesus Christ, are the focal point of God's kingdom today. Jesus taught us in the Lord's Prayer to pray, "Thy kingdom come, thy will be done, on earth as it is in heaven." To pray for the protection, blessing and success of the Church is to pray that God's kingdom would come more fully among us. The psalms read for this day provide examples of how important it is to ask God for his blessing upon his kingdom people. God's answers to these prayers provide ample reason for the people of God to sing his praise to the ends of the earth.

Exercise

Thank God that he has established his kingdom forever through Jesus Christ. And thank him that the Church, which is the body of Christ, is now the people through whom he carries out the purposes of his kingdom. Ask him to bless the Church according to some of the requests in the psalms read for today:

1. According to Psalm 20, pray that since the Church represents the kingdom of Christ on earth, God would protect it and help it in its distress (22:1), make it successful (22:4-5) and help it to stand firm (22:8).

2. According to Psalm 61, pray that God would protect the Church with his love and faithfulness (61:7).

3. According to Psalm 72, pray that the Church would be endowed with God's justice and righteousness (72:1-3), a defender/protector of the afflicted and needy and victorious over oppression (72:4), and a source of blessing to all nations (72:17).

4. According to Psalm 122, pray that the Church would be characterized by peace and prosperity (122:6-9).

If you feel led to do so, pray these same things for your own local church (or a particular church with which you are familiar). Then thank God for hearing and for responding to your prayer.

The New Testament Journey

Day 1 - Praying for Our Enemies (Matthew 5:43-48; Luke 6:27-36)

Our first passage in the New Testament leads us to a challenging aspect of intercessory prayer, namely, praying for our enemies. In Matthew, Jesus refers to what his audience has heard ("love your neighbor and hate your enemy"). This is not taken from the Old Testament but from popular but mistaken teaching of the time. Leviticus 19:18 is typical of what the Old Testament itself says: "Love your neighbor as yourself." Thus Jesus counters the popular misunderstanding of the Old Testament command by exhorting his audience to love not only their friends, but also those with whom they struggle. Examples of such people are those who persecute, hate, curse and mistreat you. Jesus says we can love such enemies by blessing them and praying for them. We have seen in our study of the Old Testament that blessing others is a way of praying for them, so the linking of these two activities is not surprising.

The motivation Jesus gives for such love is simple and profound: this is how God loves. He shows mercy to all people, sustaining their lives and waiting patiently for their repentance. As his children, should we not do the same? To do so is to see our character line up with God's character. As Matthew 5:48 makes clear, Jesus calls us to just such an alignment. We are to be perfect as our heavenly Father is perfect. In other words, we are to seek actions and attitudes that correspond to God's character, which is the measure of all that is good and right. In his gospel, Luke explains this perfection more concretely for us in a way that by now is not at all surprising. He quotes Jesus as saying we are to be merciful, as our Father in heaven is merciful (Luke 6:36). Since it is an essential aspect of God's perfect character to be merciful, alignment with his character means showing mercy.

Praying for our enemies is one key means of exhibiting God-like mercy.

Reflection

It is significant that Jesus uses intercession as a primary example of how we can love our enemies. To pray for others is an act of love. But who exactly are our enemies? And how do we pray for them?

Perhaps one of the most memorable examples answering both questions was Jesus' prayer on the cross. With death approaching, and experiencing ongoing mocking and taunting, he prayed for those who sought to destroy him, "Father, forgive them, for they do not know what they are doing" (Luke 23:34a). This incident is instructive for a number of reasons. First, it shows that even the Son of God, who loved others perfectly, was not loved by all others in return. As his disciples, we should expect the same: there will be those who respond negatively to us and the gospel we proclaim. Such people are appropriately called enemies, inasmuch as they seek to persuade us, through persecution if necessary, away from the truth of God. Second, it shows that instead of condemning such people, Jesus loved them by asking God to forgive their sinful behavior and attitudes. In this way he demonstrated alignment with God's character, since God is (as we have learned) gracious and compassionate, slow to anger and rich in love. Third, it shows us that behind the actions and attitudes of those who treat us most poorly is our true enemy, the devil. In a very real sense these people do not know what they are doing, since in some measure they have been taken captive by the evil one himself. Thus we pray for our enemies by asking God to forgive them and to set them free from the power of sin and evil in their lives.

In dealing with those who have sinned against us, and in praying for those who have been sinned against, it is important always to remember that forgiveness of others is possible only through the power of Christ in us. In her book *The Healing Presence*, Leanne Payne summarizes a personal experience of forgiving, writing, "It was as if Christ in and through me forgave the person (who can explain such a thing?) – yet I too forgave."[6] This is another instance where the symbol of the cross is invaluable. To look upon the cross and identify with the suffering of Christ there, to take our place with him and see things through his eyes, these are ways to find the spiritual power to forgive as Jesus did (and does).

Exercise

Thank God that he has revealed himself as a merciful God. Ask that you might become merciful like he is, and for the ability to pray for those who treat you poorly. Prayer for those who hate us is a difficult but Christ-like activity. Ask God to bring to mind the names of some people who might be termed enemies because of the way they treat you or respond to your faith in God. Write down their names, and pray for each of them as Jesus did: "Father, forgive them, for they do not know what they are doing." If the thought of these people raises anger or bitterness in your heart, take time to see yourself with Jesus on the cross, experiencing the hurt he did yet also forgiving those who hurt him. Ask him to forgive these people through you. Ask also that you might pray in light of the truth that "our fight is not against flesh and blood," but against the evil powers that seek to take people captive (Ephesians 6:12). Thank him for hearing and responding to your prayer.

Day 2 – The Lord's Prayer (Matthew 6:5-13; Luke 11:1-4)

Matthew gives us the Lord's Prayer in the midst of a more extended section of Jesus' teaching on prayer. It is given as a positive example or model, in contrast to the negative ones cited just before it. In it Jesus tells us "how" (not "what") to pray.

There are significant implications in this model prayer for how we are to intercede. First, the prayer is corporate. That is, it is not couched in individual terms (*my* Father) but in terms of the community of believers (*our* Father). As such it goes against our tendency to think of prayer as an individual discipline, and teaches us the importance of believers gathering together for prayer. Second, the prayer begins with worship, that is, a proper acknowledgement of the one being addressed. God is our Father, highlighting the very personal nature of his relationship with believers. His name (which stands for his essential character) is acknowledged as hallowed (or, holy), and thus we must treat him with proper reverence and submission. The prayer invites greater accomplishment of God's kingdom and of his will, on earth as it is in heaven.

It is important to grasp Jesus' teaching on the kingdom of God. God's kingdom refers to the blessing and goodness God extends to and through those who willingly submit to his reign. In the gospels, the kingdom was manifested through Jesus as he healed, cast out demons, taught truth, set prisoners free, forgave sin, etc. Matthew's term for this is "the kingdom of heaven," a term that unfortunately often makes us associate the kingdom with a place we will go in the future (i.e., to go to heaven). Jesus taught that while the full manifestation of the kingdom and all its blessings would occur in the future, it is still possible to experience now the blessings of the kingdom. Jesus' life and ministry demonstrated this present reality of the kingdom, as he healed, forgave, etc. Thus when we pray for God's kingdom to come and will be done on earth as in heaven, we are asking for a more complete experience of all the good things associated with Jesus Christ.

The Lord's Prayer ends with a series of petitions that describe some of the things marking the coming of God's kingdom in our lives. We ask for and receive daily provision, forgiveness of sin (reminding us of the need to forgive others; see Matthew 6:14-15), protection against temptation and deliverance from Satan's deceptions. The mixture of physical, emotional and spiritual petitions is a good reminder that all areas of life are appropriately committed into God's care and come under the reign of his kingdom.

Reflection

The model given to us by Jesus in the Lord's Prayer can be applied directly to intercessory prayer. Intercession is not just a task of individuals, but of the gathered body of Christ. It should begin with worship that recognizes the character of the God being addressed. This worship can occur through singing, reading of Scripture, prophecy, testimony, etc. All prayer is, in its essence, asking God to bring his kingdom more fully in this world. Intercessory prayer, in particular, asks God to manifest his kingdom more fully in another person's life. Some of the ways his kingdom is manifested are through daily provision for those who love him, the forgiveness of their sins and their forgiveness of those who sin against them, the overcoming of temptation and the setting free from the devil.

It is a good practice when you come across aspects of God's character in Scripture to make note of them by writing them down. God's character and God's kingdom go hand in hand. The coming of God's kingdom is really about his character being manifested in his people. A good way to pray for his kingdom to come in your life and the lives of others is to ask to become more like God.

Exercise

Thank God that he taught us how to pray, and that the prayer he gave us reminds us of both his holiness and his personal, fatherly concern for us. Then write down a prayer that follows the basic pattern of the Lord's Prayer. Address God as Father and honor him by stating some of his character traits, such as those found in Exodus 34:6-7. Ask him that his kingdom would come more fully today in your own life and the lives of others for whom you've been praying. Then petition God for the things listed in the Lord's Prayer: physical provision, forgiveness and the ability to forgive others, protection from Satan and his deceptions. Thank him for hearing and responding to your prayer.

Day 3 - Jesus and the Centurion (Matthew 8:5-17; Mark 1:29-34; Luke 7:1-10; John 4:46-54)

Although these passages do not mention prayer, they illustrate intercession in a very concrete way. The centurion knows (that is, believes) that Jesus has the authority and willingness to heal his servant. Thus he comes to Jesus with boldness and humility to request healing. The centurion expresses confidence that Jesus can simply speak and his paralyzed servant will be healed. Jesus extols his faith, remarking that he has not found such faith among the Jews (in John's account, the existing faith seems to grow as a result of the healing). The centurion's servant is healed immediately.

The verses that follow the story of the centurion show a similar theme. Peter's mother-in-law is healed from a fever, and all those who are sick or possessed by demons and brought to Jesus are healed. Matthew notes that the healing activity of the Messiah was foretold by the prophet Isaiah in Isaiah 53:4. We have already seen that in that same passage (Isaiah 53:12), the suffering Messiah is said to bear the sin of many, and to make intercession for transgressors. When New Testament writers such as Matthew cite verses from the Old Testament they typically have the broader context in mind (for example, when he cites Isaiah 53:4, Matthew probably has in mind Isaiah 52:13-53:12). Jesus, the Messiah, would be God's servant who would suffer death to free people from the guilt and other effects of sin. The healing of people from illness and demon possession is part of this messianic role. The cross, of course, is central to this task, since it is where Jesus accomplished the freeing from sin.

Reflection

There are two key issues for intercessory prayer in this passage. First is the emphasis on faith. Jesus draws attention to the centurion's deep trust in his ability and willingness to heal. And Jesus' response to that faith is to bring about the healing requested. Such faith is an essential part of our intercessory work. Without such confidence, we will not see prayers answered. Thus we need regularly to ask God to increase our faith ("Lord, I believe; help me in my unbelief"). Second, a fundamental act of faith is the "bringing" of people to Jesus. This is exactly what we do in intercessory prayer. Jesus is no longer present to us physically as he was during his earthly ministry, but through intercessory prayer we can approach him freely at any time and in any place. To intercede is to follow the example of the centurion and others who faithfully brought their concerns for others to Jesus so that he could address them. He is the one who lives to intercede for us (Isaiah 53:12; Romans 8:34).

It is important to realize that whereas God always hears and answers our prayers, we may not see visible results immediately. As in the Lord's Prayer, to pray for healing is to ask that God's kingdom be manifested more fully in our midst. Whether or not we see this manifestation, faith demands that we remain confident that God has heard and responded to our prayer, since this is what he has promised (see Matthew 7:7-12). Such faith also avoids the improper expectation that God must act in the way we expect. Instead, it affirms "Thy will be done," and looks expectantly and thankfully to see how God's will is accomplished in response to our prayers.

Exercise

Thank God that he responds to our prayers for others offered in faith. Ask him to help your faith grow stronger. Bring someone that needs help to Jesus, just as the centurion did. Do this by writing a prayer for this person. Follow the pattern seen in this narrative. Start with verse 6: "Lord, my friend _____ is in great need of help." Then write a paraphrase of the centurion's words as if they were your own: "Lord, I do not deserve to have you come under my roof. But just say the word, and my friend will be helped." Complete the prayer by writing a sentence expressing your confidence in Jesus to help those in need because, paraphrasing Isaiah 53:4, "You, Jesus, took up our infirmities and carried our diseases." Thank him for hearing and responding to your prayer.

Day 4 – Prayer for Harvesters (Matthew 9:35-10:1; Luke 10:1-11)

Matthew here summarizes Jesus' activities as teaching, preaching the good news of the kingdom and healing every disease and sickness. As he went through the towns and villages of Israel doing these things, he had compassion on the people he saw. They were "harassed and helpless, like sheep without a shepherd." This description tells us not only what the people of Jesus' time were experiencing, but also something of Jesus' character: he had compassion on them. We have already seen that compassion is a key attribute of God, whom Scripture describes as gracious and compassionate, slow to anger and rich in love. Thus Jesus, as God in human flesh, now exemplifies the divine character for us.

Jesus then speaks to his disciples using the analogy of a harvest. The harvest is plentiful but there are not enough disciples to work it. He urges the disciples to ask God to send workers to carry out the work of harvesting. In context, this work includes but should not be limited to evangelism, at least as we usually use the term. Strictly speaking, evangelism comes from the Greek word meaning "to bring good news," and that is exactly what Jesus desired to do for these harassed and helpless people. They needed to be taught, encouraged, healed and delivered. The work of harvest includes all of these things, driven by the compassion that Jesus himself exemplified.

We see this broader meaning of the harvest in the verses that follow. Both Matthew and Luke record Jesus sending his disciples and giving them authority over unclean spirits, and every disease and sickness. These activities demonstrate the nearness of the kingdom of God (Luke 10:9, 11). The speaking of a blessing ("Peace to this house"), which is one way to pray for others, will also bring the peace of the kingdom of God into the homes of those who are ready to receive it.

Reflection

It has been said that the gift of mercy and intercessory prayer go hand in hand. One sees in this passage why this is the case. Jesus' compassion is what drives him to invite his disciples to intercede for the masses of people. This same compassion will drive us to intercede for a world that is in deep need of God's mercy. To pray for God to send harvesters is to ask for him to supply disciples who can, like Jesus, bring the healing and helping of God's kingdom to bear on hurting lives. The immensity of the task should not discourage us, since God is clearly able and willing to provide such harvesters in response to our prayers.

Exercise

Thank God once again that he is gracious and compassionate, slow to anger and rich in love. Then write down a prayer in which you ask him, because he himself is merciful and compassionate, to demonstrate his mercy by raising up more disciples who can walk in the footsteps of Jesus by teaching, preaching the good news of the kingdom and healing people. Thank him for hearing and responding to your prayer.

Day 5 - *Jesus and the Paralytic (Matthew 9:1-8; Mark 2:1-12; Luke 5:17-26)*

The gospel writers' emphasis on Jesus' ministry of healing continues in this passage. Once again, we see someone brought to Jesus by others. In this case, friends bring a paralyzed man to Jesus, overcoming serious physical obstacles on the way. Seeing their faith (not just the man's faith), he proclaims the paralytic's sins forgiven. The Jewish leaders criticize him for this, since only God is able to forgive sins. Jesus responds by physically healing the paralytic, thus demonstrating in a tangible way his authority to forgive sins. The Jewish leaders know that no one who was blaspheming God would be able to carry out such a miracle, thus what he said about forgiving sins must be true. The crowd responds in awe and gives praise to God for giving the man Jesus such authority.

Reflection

Like the narrative about the centurion and his servant, this passage does not explicitly mention intercessory prayer. However, it does show once again the bringing of a sick person to Jesus, which is essentially what we do in intercessory prayer. No specific request is made for this man, but Jesus responds to their demonstration of faith by proclaiming him forgiven. He then heals the man's physical problems, but only as a way of demonstrating his greater authority over sin itself.

Perhaps the most significant aspect of this passage for intercessory prayer is the fact that Jesus responds to the faith of these men in what seems to be an unanticipated way. Our assumption is that the man's greatest need was to be made physically well. Jesus' addresses his spiritual condition as of primary concern. The lesson for us is once again that while

God does hear and respond to our prayers, he does so according to his wisdom and timing. In this case, and perhaps in many cases in which we have been involved, God's answer is not seen visibly but is nonetheless real and effective. Our confidence, then, must be in his ability and willingness to hear and answer, not in a particular result.

Exercise

Thank God that he sees our true needs and responds to our prayers according to those needs. Pray today that you would have faith to trust that God hears and responds to your prayers. Do this by writing out a prayer based on Hebrews 11:1: "Now faith is being sure of what we hope for and certain of what we do not see." Ask that God would make you sure and certain of these things. Then write down a situation in which you struggle to trust his response to your prayer, and ask him to increase your faith in his responsiveness. Then thank him for hearing and responding to your prayer.

Day 6 - The Ruler's Dead Daughter (Matthew 9:18-26; Mark 5:21-43; Luke 8:40-56)

Once again a person comes to Jesus with concern for someone else. This time a Jewish ruler named Jairus comes and kneels before him, saying his daughter is at the point of death. He expresses faith that, if Jesus will come and put his hand on her, she will live. Jesus goes with him and along the way the ruler's servants say it is no longer of any use, since she has died. In response Jesus exhorts the ruler, saying, "Do not fear, only believe." Entering the ruler's house, he tells the noisy mourners to leave because the girl is not dead. They laugh at him, and he proceeds to raise her from the dead.

In the midst of this narrative is the description of another significant healing. A woman who had been bleeding for a dozen years is healed after she demonstrates her faith by pursuing Jesus and touching his cloak.

Reflection

Intercessory prayer requires faith! There are so many examples in the gospels of people who, with faith, ask Jesus to help themselves and others. Jesus typically tells them their faith has made the difference. The opposite of faith is fear, and Jesus encourages the ruler (and all of us) not to fear but to trust. The response of the crowd at the ruler's house is instructive: they laughed. As with Abraham and Sarah two millennia earlier, what God says he is able to do is often beyond our comprehension. How can a barren woman past the age of childbearing have a son? And how can a dead woman live again? In both cases God demonstrates he is worthy of our faith, that he can do what seems to us impossible. No wonder the Old Testament urges us continually to "fear the LORD" and not anything else; this is the attitude from which faith springs.

Exercise

Thank God that he is able to do more than you can even comprehend. Continue to pray for faith, this time by praying against fear of anything but God. Write out the words, "Do not fear, only believe," a number of times. Each time thank the Lord for speaking these words to you, and ask him to supply the grace to make them true in your life: "O Lord, make me one who does not fear anything but You, make me one who believes. Thank You, Lord, for hearing my prayer. Amen."

Day 7 - *Jesus and the Canaanite Woman (Matthew 15:21-31; Mark 7:24-37)*

J esus here enters Gentile territory and proceeds to heal a Gentile woman's demon-possessed daughter. The woman "brings" her daughter to Jesus by crying out, "Lord, Son of David, have mercy on me!" Jesus ignores her, and his disciples urge him to send her away (perhaps by answering her plea rather than ignoring her). But the woman's faith is incessant. She cries out again, "Lord, help me!" Jesus again raises the issue of being sent to the Jewish people, and she simply and boldly replies she will accept whatever they don't receive. Certainly any crumbs off the table are more than she has! Jesus responds that her faith is great, and her daughter is immediately healed.

Jesus returns to region around the Sea of Galilee, and people continue to bring to him all in need of healing. As he heals them, the crowds respond by giving glory to God for doing such wonders.

Reflection

This woman's actions and words cut to the core of faith. She recognizes Jesus as the Jewish Messiah ("Son of David") and asks him to have mercy on her. God honors the faith of those that realize their need for his mercy. Her cry appeals to a central aspect of God's redeeming activity, that is, his desire to show compassion to a lost and needy people. Though she is not a member of God's chosen people, God's character is consistent, and her faith elicits a response of compassion from Jesus. Her prayer is answered, in that she is shown mercy in the healing of her demon possessed daughter. Once again we see the importance of faith in God's gracious and compassionate character. He shows us mercy not because we deserve it, but because it is his nature to do so.

As intercessors, we seek to emulate both the faith exhibited by this woman and the gracious character of our God.

Exercise

Thank God that he responds to those who cry out for his mercy. Continue to ask him for deeper faith. Read and write a prayer based on Hebrews 11:8-12. Express to God your desire to have faith like Abraham, trusting him to do things you can't now see or comprehend. And thank him that he has heard and responded to your prayer of faith!

Day 8 - A Man's Demon-Possessed Boy (Matthew 17:14-19; Mark 9:14-28; Luke 9:37-42)

The account of this incident is given in each of the synoptic gospels, though there are differences in emphasis. The key issue in each case is the disciples' inability to heal a demon-possessed boy due to their impoverished faith. It is hard to understand, but nonetheless apparent, that what Jesus finds disappointing is not the disciples' small faith, for he says that even small faith can do the impossible (that is, with regard to the works of the kingdom of God; Matthew 17:20-21; Luke 17:6). What Jesus finds disappointing is the quality of the disciples' faith: it is shallow, inadequate, not pure and true. Significantly, Mark connects this poor quality of faith with lack of prayer – "This kind can come out only by prayer" (Mark 9:29).

What are we to make of this? What is the difference between small faith and inadequate faith? Perhaps the best way to address the question is to ask how the disciples, who had already experienced success in casting out demons, suddenly ran into a situation they couldn't handle. And the best answer to the question is that they had begun to trust their own abilities rather than God's power. This seems to be the point of Jesus' comment recorded in Mark, that the disciples had ceased to walk in prayerful humility, and had become complacent in the authority Jesus had given them. In so doing they had cut themselves off from their true source of power. Thus prayer and faith go hand in hand, as we've already seen throughout Scripture. The disciples' failure prayerfully to depend on God indicates a loss in the quality of their faith, and this has made their prayers ineffective.

The attitude of the boy's father is described in greatest detail in Mark's account. He comes to Jesus and says, "If you can do anything, take pity on us and help us" (9:22). This cry for help is consistent with the pleas of others such as the Canaanite woman ("Lord, Son of David, have mercy on me!"), and reminds us that prayer in such matters is always an appeal to God's merciful character. Jesus uses the man's words, "if you can," to make the point that his ability to heal is beyond question. What is at issue is the faith of the one asking. The man humbly responds to Jesus with a statement that shows the tension all of us face with regard to trusting God: "I do believe; help me overcome my unbelief!"

It is worth noting that Jesus sends the demon away with a command. This is another example of the manifestation of the kingdom of God among us. Jesus is the King of God's kingdom, and has been given all authority by the Father. The demons have no choice but to respond to his command. We too, as his disciples, have such authority when we trust in his power and call humbly upon his name.

Reflection

It should be clear by now that bringing others to Jesus for help and healing requires faith. Our God is not bound to respond to us simply because we say the right words or go through the correct motions. Active faith is required, as we would expect and desire for intercession that flows out of a personal relationship with God. Such faith is not the same as trusting in our own God-given abilities, or in our past successes. It is about an ongoing attitude of dependence on God, and confidence in his authority and power as revealed in his Word, and experienced in our lives. As Jesus says in Mark 9:29, prayer is a vital and necessary way of expressing such faith.

Exercise

Thank God that he has given Jesus authority over all things in heaven and on earth. Then pray (and make a habit of praying) using the words found in these and other passages in the gospels. First, when you pray for yourself or someone else, begin by writing down the words, "Lord, have mercy on me!" After writing down the situation or name of the person you are praying for and what you are asking, finish your prayer by writing the words, "Lord, I do believe; help me in my unbelief!" Then thank God for hearing and responding to your prayer and maturing your faith.

Day 9 - James and John and Their Place in the Kingdom (Matthew 20:20-28; Mark 10:35-45; cf. Luke 22:24-27)

The account of James and John's request for priority of place in Jesus' kingdom follows immediately after an honest prophecy of Jesus' imminent death (Matthew 20:17-19; Mark 10:32-34). Apparently these two and their mother do not understand that Jesus' kingdom is not so much about individual power as about service, including suffering. The mother of the two men brings them to Jesus to request that they might have high standing in his kingdom, sitting at his right and left hand. Jesus tells them they do not know what they are asking (that is, for suffering and servant-hood, not authority over others), and that such standing in the kingdom is, in any case, not his to give. This privilege belongs to the Father alone.

Reflection

Two key lessons are taught about intercession in this narrative. First, the failure of these three characters to understand illustrates that we must always maintain a stance of humility towards God's plans and purposes. We do not have the same complete perspective on our requests as he does. The words of the Lord's prayer, "Thy will be done," are ever so important here – much better for us that God's good and gracious will be done rather than our will, since our will is based on limited understanding and mixed motives. Second, we are reminded that even Jesus' authority comes not from himself, but from the Father. Any authority given to us is similarly derivative, and we deceive ourselves if we think that we have earned such authority, or that it is an intrinsic part of our character. Just as the Father granted Jesus authority, so he grants authority to us through Jesus, according to his perfect will and plan. Only with such an understanding, exemplified for us by Jesus, can we exhibit the true humility and servant-hood to which Jesus calls us. Intercessory prayer is one way we may serve, and even suffer, for Christ and his kingdom.

Exercise

Thank God that he is the source of our spiritual authority, just as he was the source of Jesus' spiritual authority. Write a prayer for yourself based on Matthew 20:25-28. In your prayer ask God that you might, like Jesus, be one who seeks greatness not through gaining and using authority over others as the rulers of the Gentiles did, but through becoming a servant to others. Thank God for hearing and responding to your prayer.

Day 10 - Jesus and the Blind Man at Bethsaida (Mark 8:22-30)

This passage is unique in the gospels in that it shows Jesus performing a healing that is not instantaneous. As in so many passages, others bring someone in need of healing to Jesus, who uses physical touch to heal. After the second touch, the man's eyes are opened and his sight fully restored. Mark has placed this incident immediately before Peter's confession of Jesus as the Christ (that is, the expected Old Testament Messiah). This placement is probably to highlight the similarities between the physical blindness of the man, and the spiritual blindness of the many that do not recognize who Jesus really is.

Reflection

Two key issues regarding intercessory prayer come to our attention in this passage. One is the possibility of gradual or stepwise answers to our prayers. The healing of the blind man does not occur instantaneously, and many times God's answer to our prayers will not be immediately apparent. This does not mean that we lack faith or that God is not hearing and responding. John Calvin, the great sixteenth century reformer, believed that this stepwise healing showed that God is truly free in how he responds to our prayers. Jesus has what John Calvin called "full liberty" in the way he heals, and sometimes his healing moves like a slow, steady stream rather than a raging rapids. These are important points to remember when we pray for others. God is the one who heals, and he does it in his way and in his time. Once again, our faith is in his hearing and responding, not in how he will answer.

The second key issue is the comparison of physical with spiritual blindness. God is able and willing to heal both types of blindness. As intercessors, it is important to pray not just for obvious physical needs. We must also ask that God would, for example lift spiritual misunderstanding from a person. Such misunderstanding can keep a person from experiencing the many healing benefits of the kingdom of God. Paul's prayers, such as Ephesians 1:17-19, often appeal to God to help believers "see" spiritual reality more clearly. We can feel confident in praying the same, and we will see specific ways of doing so when we study Paul's prayers.

Exercise

Thank God that he is free to respond to our prayers according to his own wisdom and timing, and that he knows our true needs. Pray that he would give you patience and faith to accept his sovereign will with regard to your prayers. Pray also that he would help you to see beyond the physical into the spiritual realm, and to be able to pray accordingly. Thank him that he has given you the Holy Spirit to help you in this task. Finally, thank God for hearing and responding to your prayer.

Day 11 - Jesus and Lazarus (John 11:1-45)

John tells us here of another incident in which people brought someone in need to Jesus. This time it is Mary and Martha who bring their sick brother Lazarus. Jesus is away, and they send word to him, saying, "Lord, the one you love is sick." Jesus responds by saying that Lazarus' sickness, which will not end in death, is for God's glory. He does not rush off to heal Lazarus, but surprisingly remains where he is for two more days. By the time he leaves, Lazarus has died, and Jesus tells his disciples this happened that they might believe.

When Jesus arrives at Bethany, Martha goes out to meet him and utters a wonderfully insightful statement of faith in Jesus: "Lord, if you had been here, my brother would not have died. But I know that even now God will give you whatever you ask." Her sincere confidence is what F. B. Meyer calls "the fulcrum of faith on which to rest the lever of (Christ's) mighty power."[7] Mary makes a similar statement when she meets Jesus, and the passage describes his deep compassion in response to her and others' weeping. Jesus reminds Martha of what he had told her, that if she believed she would see the glory of God. He then prays to the Father, first thanking him for hearing his prayer. He says this aloud so that those present will believe the Father truly sent him. When he is finished, Jesus calls out to Lazarus, who comes forth covered in grave clothes.

Reflection

This story, like so many we have read, demonstrates the beautiful combination of compassion and power that Jesus exemplified. As Martha sees, he is the one who can ask for and receive amazing things from the Father. And as Jesus shows, his compassion is real. He reacts with heartfelt emotion to his friends' loss, and responds to their plight by restoring their lost brother. This is the same Jesus to whom we bring our friends' needs.

Exercise

Thank God that he showed us, through his son Jesus, the deep love he has for us, a love that led Jesus to weep over the suffering of his friends. Compassion was so vital to Jesus' ministry, and it is vital to intercessory ministry. Continue to ask God that you might be like Jesus in having compassion on those who are needy. And ask him to help you continue to respond to the needs of others by faithfully bringing them to Jesus in prayer. Thank him for hearing and responding to your prayer.

Day 12 - Jesus and His Followers (John 17)

This prayer is different than all we have seen so far, since in it Jesus himself intercedes at length. In his prayer, he brings those who believe in him to the Father. The prayer begins with Jesus looking up into heaven. As he prays, he rehearses the reasons he came to earth. He asks the Father to glorify him, so that the Father might likewise be glorified. He restates the authority given to him by the Father, namely to give eternal life to those the Father has given him. This life comes through knowing the Father, who is the only true God, and knowing the Son whom the Father sent.

Jesus then prays for the ones the Father has given him "out of the world." Throughout his prayer we sense an upward movement. He is still among his followers, but he is already moving back to the Father. Thus he prays for their protection from the world's evil, a protection that enables the disciples to enjoy on earth the same unity that the Father, Son and Holy Spirit enjoy in heaven.

This unity is an essential and newly revealed part of God's character. He exists in three persons in perfect relationship with one another (see, for example, John 16:13-15). The revelation of this aspect of God's character seems to be what Jesus refers to as the "name" that God gave to him, a "name" that Jesus then also revealed to his disciples (17:6, 11): God, as Father, Son, and Holy Spirit, is perfect in unity. To pray according to God's "name" is to pray in light of his essential character, which as Jesus now reveals includes perfect unity. Jesus then shows us just what praying according to God's name or character means. He asks that God, who is defined by perfect unity, would bring the same supernatural unity among his followers.

Jesus then prays that the disciples might have a full measure of his joy within them. This joy is linked to their new identity in Jesus, rather than to the world of which they are no longer a part. Jesus prays again for protection from the evil one, asking that the Father would sanctify them through his word of truth. This sanctification refers to the "setting apart" of the disciples for the God-given task of bringing the world to Christ. Just as the Father gave Jesus the special mission of going into the world, so Jesus now prays that the disciples might be given by God the special mission of going into the world. Jesus asks that they might be successful in their mission just as he was (17:4).

Jesus widens the focus of his prayer to include those who will come to the Father through the successful mission of the disciples. He asks for unity, a unity once again stemming from their relationship with the Father through Jesus. In a very real sense, believers are lifted up into the heavenly relationship of the Trinity. The resulting unity will be a witness to the world that the Father sent Jesus, and that he now gives the same love he has for Jesus to those who follow Christ. As singer and songwriter Sandra McCracken, writes of the Father, "No less than your love for Jesus is mine."[8]

Reflection

This passage is so rich with teaching about God that it's easy to lose sight of what it says about intercession. Yet in a sense, that is why the passage is so powerful and relevant. The truth is that we cannot separate our prayers from our understanding of who God is, and what his purpose is for believers. To pray apart from such understanding is to fail to pray according to God's will and character.

So what does this passage teach about God and his purpose for believers? First, that God desires believers to live out their lives in the context of this world. He does not ask them to escape, but to learn to function among those in the world without being like them. Second, God desires believers to live in a way that reflects God's own character. Jesus exemplified this character while he was on earth, living in perfect unity with the Father and with those who followed him. Joy characterized this unity, along with a sense of mission that the world could not understand or reproduce. This loving unity was what drew people to the Father through Jesus.

When we pray for other believers, one of our fundamental prayers must be for unity. This is not a prayer for administrative unity or a vague feeling of togetherness. Rather, it is a prayer that the very character of God would be exemplified in the people of God. In this way, God will draw those in "the world" to himself, and the church of God will fulfill its God-given mission. For the church to be successful, God must protect it from the evil one, who seeks to create division, dissension and despair among God's people.

Exercise

Begin by thanking God that he has brought you into relationship with himself through Jesus. Then pray for unity for believers throughout the world in the following way.

1.   Praise God that he exists forever in perfect unity of the Father, the Son and the Holy Spirit.

2.   Ask him to bring the same unity among followers of Christ that exists among the Father, Son and Holy Spirit.
      a.   Pray for believers everywhere, that they might experience Jesus' joy.

b.   Pray for believers everywhere, that God will protect them from the deceptions of the evil one, who seeks to bring about disunity.

c.   Pray for believers everywhere, that they might understand and act upon their mission, as those sent into the world by God to bring those in the world back to God.

3.   Give thanks to God that he has heard your requests, and that he is bringing about a unity that reveals the love God has within himself, and the love he has for the church.

Day 13 - Stephen and His Persecutors (Acts 7:54-8:1)

Stephen is a believer who was part of the early church in Jerusalem. Acts 6:5-8 describes him as "a man full of faith and of the Holy Spirit," and "a man full of God's grace and power" who "did great wonders and miraculous signs among the people." His effective ministry attracted persecution, and the Jewish authorities arrested him and false witnesses brought accusations against him. With his "face like the face of an angel" (6:15), Stephen preached a fiery sermon that ended by calling his audience a "stiff-necked people, with uncircumcised hearts and ears," who "always resist the Holy Spirit." Those present responded by stoning him to death. His intercession for those who were stoning him came just before he died, "Lord, do not hold this sin against them."

Reflection

Stephen's intercession is reminiscent of Jesus' prayer on the cross, "Father, forgive them, for they do not know what they are doing" (Luke 23:24). Both prayers represent a truly God-like attitude. It is not natural for us to seek to bless those who bring us pain. Yet this is a central quality of God's love revealed in Jesus, a love that loves not only those who love back, but even those who hate and persecute. Stephen's prayer is another example to us of how our intercession must express God's gracious character. Rather than praying God's judgment on those who persecute us, we ask that he might show them the same mercy he has shown each of us.

Exercise

Begin by thanking God that he is a merciful God, and that he has shown you mercy in particular situations (list some, being as specific as possible). Then ask him to show similar mercy to someone whom you have difficulty loving. If this person is simply hard for you to like, pray that God would allow you to see and deal with this person as God does (that is, mercifully). If this person has sinned against you, try to pray Stephen's words: "Lord, do not hold this sin against them." It is important once again to remember that the power truly to forgive those who have sinned against us comes only through Christ himself. Ask God to let you know in the depths of your soul the forgiveness that he extends to that person through Christ. Thank him for hearing and responding to your prayer.

Day 14 - The Samaritans and the Holy Spirit (Acts 8:9-23, 9:10-19 & 19:1-7)

The stoning of Stephen led to a more general persecution of the Christians in Jerusalem. All but the apostles were scattered from Jerusalem into the surrounding regions of Judea and Samaria. The latter was, of course, where the much-hated Samaritans lived. When Samaritans began to accept the gospel, the apostles sent Peter and John to them. They prayed for the Samaritan believers that they might receive the Holy Spirit, and when Peter and John placed their hands on them, the Holy Spirit came.

Paul (also known as Saul) was one of the persecutors who caused believers to scatter. His encounter with Jesus on the road to Damascus changed him forever. Ananias was a disciple used by God to release Paul from his spiritual blindness. When he laid hands on Paul and told him that Jesus intended to restore his sight, scales fell from Paul's eyes and he was filled with the Holy Spirit and baptized.

As the Lord had told Ananias, Paul became one of the gospel's chief messengers, bringing its message of hope and restoration to people in Asia Minor and Europe. In Acts 19, he is returning from his second journey to Europe, and he comes to the city of Ephesus in Asia Minor. Finding some disciples, he inquires as to the nature of their baptism and whether they had received the Holy Spirit. Their baptism was that of John the Baptist, and Paul explains that John was a forerunner of Jesus. Paul then baptizes them into the name of the Lord Jesus. When he places his hands on them, they receive the Holy Spirit and begin to speak in tongues and prophesy.

Reflection

These passages together present a general model for praying for the Holy Spirit. Scripture is clear that this is a prayer God delights to answer. For example, Luke (who also wrote Acts) quotes Jesus in his gospel, "If you then, though you are evil, know how to give good gifts to your children, how much more will your Father give the Holy Spirit to those who ask him!" (Luke 11:13) Jesus promised that believers would be given the gift of the Spirit (Acts 1:4, 8), and in the passages read today, the filling of the Spirit marks the beginning of the new life in Christ for these believers. Elsewhere in Scripture, believers are exhorted to continue being filled with the Spirit, so the usefulness of such prayer extends beyond the initial encounter with Christ.

In each of the passages, the one praying lays hands on those who receive the gift of the Spirit. Why is the giving of the Spirit associated with the laying on of hands? Is this to be seen as a necessary aspect of prayer for the Holy Spirit? We will see other cases in which believers use the laying on of hands, apart from prayer, for the coming of the Holy Spirit. Thus, this action has a broader application than verbalized intercessory prayer. However, the laying on of hands seems to be an important aspect of the prayer for the Holy Spirit. Most likely it is a symbolic gesture, which highlights the connection between the one praying and the one receiving prayer and, more generally, between these two and the broader body of Christ. As we saw in John 17, God intends his own character to become incarnate in his body, the church. Laying on hands while praying illustrates the way God extends his healing and helping character to others through those who pray. In each of these passages, those who had received the Holy Spirit mediated him to those who hadn't.

In the Acts 19 passage, though prayer is not mentioned explicitly, external signs such as speaking in tongues and prophesying accompany the initiation. It would be pressing the passage too far to say that such signs will always be present when believers receive the gift of the Spirit. However, such signs are clearly a legitimate indication of God's response to prayer for his Spirit.

Finally, it is important, when speaking about the work of the Holy Spirit, to remember Jesus' own words in John 3:8:

> The wind blows wherever it pleases. You hear its sound, but you cannot tell where it comes from or where it is going. So it is with everyone born of the Spirit.

Attempting to lock the Spirit's work into a particular pattern is like trying to capture the wind in a box. We must respect the Holy Spirit's sovereign movements and pray with proper humility and submission for the Spirit to do his work among us. We can be certain, however, that the Holy Spirit is a special gift given to all believers in Jesus Christ (Romans 8:9b – "And if anyone does not have the Spirit of Christ, he does not belong to Christ;" see also John 3:5-6). We can also be certain that the Christian life depends upon our willingness to be responsive to the Holy Spirit's activity in our hearts. The authors of Scripture use a variety of terms to refer to this responsiveness ("living in accordance with the Spirit" (Romans 8:5); "being led by the Spirit" (Galatians 5:18); "keeping in step with the Spirit" (Galatians 5:25); "being filled with the Spirit" (Ephesians 5:18)). The essential exhortation is the same in each case: let God do his work in you by means of his Holy Spirit. Like the wind, the Spirit himself is not visible, but the effects of his work in us will be.

Exercise

Thank God that he sent his Holy Spirit to take Jesus' place with us when Jesus returned to the Father. Then ask God to help you to be responsive to his Spirit, using some of the phrases the authors of Scripture use. For example, ask God to help you to live in accordance with the Spirit. Then ask him to help you to keep in step with the Spirit, etc. Ask that the effects of his Spirit's work would be evident in your life, and ask God for a fresh infilling of the Spirit. Pray the same thing for others that God brings to mind. Thank him for hearing and responding to your prayer.

Day 15 – Peter, Aeneas and Dorcas (Acts 9:32-43; 20:7-12; 28:1-10)

In the first passage, Peter plays the role of healer just as Jesus did when he was on earth. He heals a man who had been bedridden for eight years, a healing that leads many to turn to the Lord. Then some believers bring Peter to a room that contains the deceased body of a beloved believer named Tabitha. Peter sends those present out of the room, just as Jesus had done with Jairus' daughter, then commands Tabitha to get up. This she does, and many more believe in the Lord because of her healing.

In Acts 20, Paul's long preaching leads a young man to fall to his death from a third story window. Paul puts his arm around the dead man, and he is immediately restored to life. Then in chapter 28 Paul heals the father of a Maltese official named Publius. This last healing occurs through prayer followed by the laying on of hands. It leads many others on the island to come to Paul and receive healing.

Reflection

Prayer is not mentioned specifically in any of these passages, yet they still illustrate the way Peter and Paul were given the same authority to heal as Jesus was. It is wrong to assume that these men were granted this power because they were some sort of super-Christians. The point of these passages is to show that Jesus' words to his disciples were coming true: "I tell you the truth, anyone who has faith in me will do what I have been doing. He will do even greater things than these, because I am going to the Father" (John 14:12; see also Acts 5:12-16).

As intercessors, there is a sense in which we too follow in the healing footsteps of Jesus. We are now God's hands, his body, empowered by his Holy Spirit to bring healing in Jesus' name. This is not to say that Jesus is out of the picture. Quite the contrary, since Jesus himself said that our ability to heal like he did depends upon our faith in him. He is the healer, and he desires to mediate his healing power through those who believe in him. As intercessors we simply bring this healing power to bear on the needs of others.

Prayer for healing, whether physical or emotional, is both mysterious and controversial. Scripture is clear that Jesus came to heal, and that he gave his followers the same task. Faith is always central to effective healing prayer, whether it is faith on the part of the one praying, the one being prayed for, or the ones who bring someone for healing prayer. We must be careful not to expect that all healing prayer will have results such as those described in this passage. However, we are still called to cooperate in faith with God's healing purposes. How exciting it will be to see him use us as his instruments to bring healing to those for whom we pray.

Exercise

Thank God that he is a God of healing, and that he heals today just as he did 2,000 years ago. Thank him also that he has chosen to use people like you to carry out his healing purposes. Ask him to give you the faith to trust that he can heal through your prayers. Ask him also to show you clearly if and when there are people for whom you should pray for healing. Thank him for hearing and responding to your prayer.

Day 16 - The Church's Earnest Prayer for Peter (Acts 12:1-19)

In this passage, Peter is arrested for his faith and put into prison. The church, which included at the very least those who were praying at Mary's house, was "earnestly praying to God for him." The translation "earnestly" reflects a word that in Greek means to "stretch out," the sense being that the believers were engaged in serious prayer characterized by lying prostrate or with hands continually raised to heaven. This prayer went on for days while Herod waited for the Passover festival to end. The night before Herod intended to bring him to trial, Peter was miraculously set free. When he realized what had happened, he understood the Lord had set him free by sending an angel. When Peter arrived at Mary's house, the believers there were so astonished that at first they didn't believe it was him. Peter gave credit to the Lord for saving him, implying a strong link between the believer's prayers and his deliverance.

Reflection

Do the fervent prayers made by a group of believers really matter? This passage certainly suggests so. From the human point of view, Peter's situation was hopeless. James, the brother of John, had already been put to death, and Peter's execution seemed imminent. To escape from a heavily guarded prison seemed impossible. Yet the church gathered and earnestly prayed, and God responded by setting Peter free. Luke highlights for us the role that prayer played by mentioning, both before and after the story of Peter's escape, the fact that the church was interceding for him. Once again, God does the impossible in response to the prayers of his people.

It is easy to make intercessory prayer an individual activity. Our culture has so emphasized the individual that we have often lost sight of the value and power of community life. This passage beautifully illustrates the impact of a church committed to praying for others in need. When believers gather to intercede, they encourage each other in the often difficult task of persevering in prayer.

Exercise

Thank God that he has created the church to be a community in which believers can gather to worship and encourage one another in the life of faith. Ask God to raise up within your church those who will pray together for others' needs. If your church already has such a group, pray that God would bring more people to pray, that he would protect the group from the evil one, and that the group would grow deeper in faith and fervency. Thank God for hearing and responding to your prayer.

Day 17 - Praying for Leaders (Acts 13:1-3; 14:21-25)

B oth Barnabas and Paul (or Saul) belonged to the church at Antioch in Syria. While they and other teachers and prophets were worshiping and fasting, the Holy Spirit spoke to them and told them to set apart these two men for the work to which God had called them. With fasting and praying and the laying on of hands, the church sent Barnabas and Paul to preach the gospel to people who hadn't yet heard it. Many responded to the gospel as Paul and Barnabas traveled the cities and towns of Asia Minor. As the two men retraced their steps they encouraged the disciples in each place, and appointed elders to lead them. Paul and Barnabas committed these elders with prayer and fasting to the Lord, "in whom they had put their trust."

Reflection

These passages illustrate some interesting features of intercessory prayer. In the first passage, God's direction to set apart Paul and Barnabas comes in response to the worship and fasting of the leaders of the Antioch church. The receptive posture taken by these leaders made it possible for them to receive the Spirit's guidance. Once this direction was received, the leaders responded with more fasting, prayer for Paul and Barnabas and the laying on of hands. The content of the prayer is not given, but probably centered on asking God for protection, provision and success in the work to which he had called Paul and Barnabas. The laying on of hands, as we've already seen, is a powerful symbol of the way God extends his power and blessing through Christ to the body of Christ and to the individual members of the body. In the same way he became incarnate in Jesus Christ, so now through Jesus he becomes incarnate in the body of Christ.

Thus the laying on of hands is an important symbol of his real presence in and among his people.

Paul and Barnabas pray and fast when they commission leaders in the churches they have planted in Asia Minor. Luke does not describe how they chose leaders, so we cannot say for certain that the situation was the same as in Acts 13. However, the description of intercessory prayer and fasting shows that these practices were often linked in the early church.

Exercise

Thank God that he speaks to us through his Holy Spirit. Then ask the Lord to show you an issue or situation in which you and others can seek his direction. Ask others to join you in seeking God's guidance. Consider fasting for a time, especially with other believers who will pray with you. And be sure to begin your time of prayer together with worship. You can do this by singing songs of praise and thanksgiving, by reading psalms such as Psalm 34 or Psalm 118, or by taking turns recounting to him his wonderful attributes ("Lord, You are merciful, compassionate, gracious, loving, gentle," etc.). Commit time and energy to being open to listen to what the Lord says. Thank him for hearing and responding to your request.

Day 18 - The Seven Sons of Sceva (Acts 19:11-20)

This fascinating passage describes the misguided attempt of some Jewish sorcerers to tap into the power of Jesus Christ. Paul was having great success, as "God did extraordinary miracles" through him. The seven sons of Sceva, who is described as a Jewish chief priest, were among those mimicking Paul and commanding demons to come out in the name of Jesus. One day an evil spirit responded to them, admitting the power of Jesus and Paul but wondering mockingly who they thought they were. The man with the evil spirit physically overpowered them and sent them running. The result was that many Jews and Greeks living near Ephesus came to esteem Jesus, with some turning publicly from their sorcery. As Luke notes, "the word of the Lord spread widely and grew in power."

Reflection

Luke here reminds us of the danger of unbelief. In the gospels, and all of Scripture, faith is essential to the practice of intercessory prayer. Our tendency is to want to try more diligently to believe, which is an appropriate response and a good motivation for calling on the Lord's help ("Lord, I believe; help me in my unbelief"). However, what we see in this passage is true unbelief. These men were attempting to invoke the power of Jesus name apart from faith in Jesus, and the result is disastrous. Thus the passage serves both as an encouragement and a warning to us. It is encouraging because it helps us to realize that, however we might struggle to believe, we are still working from a standpoint of acceptance of and confidence in Jesus. That is, as believers in Christ we are on the right side of the fence. The warning is that Jesus' name is not a magical part of an incantation formula. In contrast to much misguided teaching, it is not enough simply to say Jesus' name when we pray. We must, with the Holy Spirit's help, also put our trust in the person behind the name. In fact, such trust precedes the use of the name; apart from confidence in Jesus himself, the use of his name is mere superstition.

Exercise

Thank God that he has brought you into his kingdom through faith, and given you the Holy Spirit. Thank him that he accepts your desire and your attempts to trust him fully. Ask him to give you deeper faith in his son Jesus, faith that enables you to be a part of the growth of his kingdom. Confess to him any times you might have used the name of Jesus superstitiously, without accompanying faith. And thank him for the forgiveness he gives you, and for hearing and responding to your prayer.

Day 19 - Paul and the Church at Rome (Romans 1:1-17)

T his is the first letter of Paul we come to in reading the New Testament. Paul begins this letter with a description of his calling as an apostle (a messenger specially appointed by God) to the Gentiles. As is his custom, he then blesses the Roman believers (1:7). Such a blessing is, as we've seen, a form of intercession since it asks God to act on behalf of those being blessed. Paul reports his thanksgiving for the renown of the Roman church, and says God is his witness to the way he constantly remembers the Romans in his prayers. His prayer now, he says, is that God will allow him to come to see them.

Why is it important that he visit the Roman believers? Paul explains that he desires that he and they may be mutually encouraged by each other's faith. He also speaks of having a "harvest" among them, as he has had among other Gentiles. This thought leads Paul to proclaim the essence of the gospel he proclaims. In this gospel "a righteousness from God is revealed, a righteousness that is by faith from first to last" (1:17).

Reflection

Paul's letters make clear that he was a man of prayer. As in many other passages, Paul here refers both to the regularity of his prayers for others (he prays for the Romans constantly), and to their content (his desire to come to Rome to encourage the believers and lead others to Christ). This desire to come to Rome is motivated by his calling as an apostle to Gentiles. His persistence in this prayer is indicated by his reference to the many times he had been providentially hindered from such a visit (1:13).

Paul's description of his prayers demonstrates an interesting aspect of intercessory prayer. On the surface, his request to go to Rome could be seen as a personal, idiosyncratic or even selfish desire. Yet this request, and the desire behind it, stem from his God-given calling to bring the gospel to the Gentile world, of which Rome was the center. Thus his calling led to a desire that was quite specific, namely, visiting a particular people in a particular place. This desire, coupled with faith in the God who gave it, led Paul to intercede continuously for the Roman church and for the opportunity to visit them.

God has also called each of us to certain peoples in certain places and times. Though we may not always be aware like Paul was of our specific calling, we can trust that God has put desires in our hearts that reflect this calling. Unfortunately, many of us have been taught to ignore our heart's desires since we think they must inevitably be selfish. A better approach, and the one illustrated here by Paul, is to lay our desires before God. Paul's deep desire to visit the Roman church did not fade after repeated setbacks, so Paul brought his desire before God again and again. Interestingly, though this letter doesn't record God's answer to his prayers, the book of Acts describes his eventual arrival in Rome where he lived for two years under house arrest. During this time, he welcomed all who came to see him, and "boldly and without hindrance he preached the kingdom of God and taught about the Lord Jesus Christ" (Acts 28:31). Thus Paul's persistence was rewarded, though perhaps not in the exact way he might have planned!

Exercise

Thank God that he calls us to contribute in unique ways to the growth of his kingdom. Thank him also that he gives us desires that help drive us to fulfill our calling. What are your deep desires? Following Paul's example, write your deepest yearnings down and lay them before God. Are there desires that you've quenched because you were discouraged when they weren't fulfilled? Lay these before God, and by faith ask God to fulfill them and to remove desires that he has not given. Ask him to give you the faith required to continue pursuing in prayer the desires he has given you. Then thank God for hearing and responding to your prayer.

Day 20 - Paul and the Romans, Part 2 (Romans 15:14-33)

T owards the end of his letter, Paul again expresses his desire to visit the city of Rome. This time he explains in greater detail his plans, which include delivering a gift of money to the poor believers in Jerusalem and then stopping in Rome on his way to Spain. He also reiterates his motivation, namely, to fulfill his calling "to preach the gospel where Christ was not known." Since the eastern Mediterranean area has been reached with the gospel, Paul is ready to head west to those who haven't yet heard the good news. Paul asks the Roman church to pray for his protection from opponents in Jerusalem, and for his gift of money to be acceptable to the Jerusalem church. Then he will be able to come to them with joy and for mutual encouragement.

Reflection

This passage is instructive both for its clarifying of Paul's situation and for the way Paul asks the Roman believers to intercede on his behalf. His desire to visit Rome is still apparent, although it becomes clear that he has set his sights even further west toward Spain. His inability to visit them thus far has been due to his preaching "from Jerusalem all the way around to Illyricum" (that is, the eastern Mediterranean region). Having completed that task, he plans to return to Jerusalem to deliver money given by believers in Asia and Europe to help the poor saints in Jerusalem. Then, he believes, he will be able to visit the Roman believers in the "full measure of the blessing of Christ."

Paul urges the Roman believers "by our Lord Jesus Christ and by the love of the Spirit." In light of their relationship to Christ, and in light of all Christ has granted to them through his Holy Spirit, is it not appropriate to expect them to pray for the success of his service to Christ? In particular, Paul wants them to join him in his struggle. What a fascinating picture! Paul, who clearly has some legitimate fears about how he will be received by believers and non-believers in Jerusalem, invites the Roman church to enter the struggle with him by praying for him. We are reminded of Paul's words in Ephesians 6:12 that "our struggle is not against flesh and blood, but against the rulers, against the authorities, against the powers of this dark world and against the spiritual forces of evil in the heavenly realms." Paul asks the Roman Christians, as a response to the love of Christ poured out for them, to join him in this very battle using the weapons of the Spirit, especially prayer. Intercessory prayer is seen here in serious and sacrificial terms.

Paul asks the Romans to pray for two things. The first is deliverance from Jews who would persecute him in Jerusalem (remember: Paul was a Christian-hating Jew who became a Christian hated by Jews). The second is acceptance of his gift by the Jerusalem church (Paul's Christian-hating activities had not been forgotten, and his association with Gentiles still made some Jewish Christians wary). With these prayers answered, he would be able finally to enjoy the refreshment of fellowship with the Roman church and then continue on to preach the gospel in Spain.

Interestingly, Paul's prayers each received a different sort of answer. He was imprisoned by unbelievers in Jerusalem, accepted by the believers there, and came (as we noted above) to Rome as a prisoner. We have no compelling evidence that he ever made it to Spain.

Exercise

Thank God that through prayer, which is a spiritual activity, you can join the struggles of other believers no matter how far away. Continue to pray regarding your deepest desires. Paul was willing to suffer great physical, emotional and spiritual trials to see his God-given desires fulfilled. Ask God once again for wisdom to discern what desires he has given you. Ask him for patience and persistence in praying for these desires to be fulfilled. As is appropriate, ask him for guidance on having others pray for you regarding your sense of calling, just as Paul asked the Roman believers to join his struggle. Thank God for hearing and responding to your prayer.

Day 21 - The Intercession of the Holy Spirit (Romans 8:18-27)

This passage is the first to describe the intercessory role of the Holy Spirit. The context in this part of Paul's letter to the Romans is the suffering that inevitably accompanies the life of faith in Christ. We groan inwardly as we wait for our salvation to be completed, with our adoption as God's children and the redemption of our bodies. In fact, all of creation groans, as it longs for freedom from the decay and bondage caused by sin. For now, we must continue on in hope, as Paul emphasizes through repetition in 8:24-25. Hope in our eventual redemption is the antidote to the sufferings we presently face. Paul writes that "the Spirit helps us in our weakness." The word for weakness is a general term, and can refer to any need or problem associated with our life in this world. Though we don't always know just what to pray concerning our weaknesses, Paul says the Holy Spirit prays on our behalf. Paul's logic is that just as our future hope is the answer to our present sufferings, so the intercessory ministry of the Spirit is the answer to our present weakness.

Reflection

How does the Spirit help us in our weakness? Even though we don't know just what to pray for, the Spirit prays for our needs with perfect knowledge of us and of God's will. The Spirit prays "with groans that words cannot express." The exact nature of this groaning is not specified. However, what is clear is that the Spirit works at a level beyond reason, so that we need not have a rational understanding of his intercession. Some have linked this non-rational intercession with speaking in tongues, so that the believer who prays in tongues is communicating directly through the Spirit apart from the rational mind. This may be what Paul means by "praying in the Spirit" in Ephesians 6:18. The value of such a mode of prayer is obvious, since it is not subject to the limitations and errors of interpretation that our reason and emotions often bring to the task of prayer. Prayer in the Spirit is essentially God-speaking to himself on our behalf, as the Spirit makes known to the Father (who searches our hearts) our true needs.

Later in this same chapter of Romans, Paul reminds us that Jesus himself is "at the right hand of God and is also interceding for us" (8:34; see also Hebrews 7:25). This means that the second and third members of the Trinity (the Son and the Holy Spirit) are both praying for believers according to God's will. That's some pretty significant prayer support! The intercessory role of the Holy Spirit is less emphasized in the New Testament, but Paul reminds us here of the utter intimacy of the Spirit's ministry on our behalf. Thanks to God for providing this intercession for us!

Exercise

Thank God that he lives in you through his Holy Spirit. Thank him also that this same Spirit prays for all believers in their weakness. Thank him that even though you don't always know what to pray, the Spirit intercedes for you and other believers with full knowledge of your true needs and of God's will. And thank God that you do not have to understand what is prayed in order for it to be effective.

Day 22 - Paul and the Corinthians (2 Corinthians 1:1-11)

P aul begins what is known as the second letter to the Corinthians with a focus on God's comfort in the midst of great suffering. Paul and his missionary companions suffered tremendous physical and emotional hardships, at times literally risking their lives. Yet God had used these sufferings to make them more dependent upon him, and to enable them to bring comfort to the Corinthian believers as they too suffered for their faith. God had been faithful to deliver Paul and his companions, and Paul expresses confidence that God will continue to deliver them, as the Corinthian believers pray for such deliverance. The result of their deliverance will be the giving of thanks for God's gracious answer to these prayers.

Reflection

Paul here asks for the Corinthian believers to intercede for him and his companions. They had successfully brought the gospel to those who hadn't heard, but in the process had elicited great resentment. The book of Acts describes the hostile reaction of many to the gospel, and the physical abuse that Paul and others received at the hands of their persecutors. They were accosted, driven out of towns and even stoned and left for dead because of their preaching. Paul expresses his hope that God will continue to keep them safe. He then indicates that the Corinthian believers actually help him in this hope of deliverance as they pray.

Paul seems quite comfortable asking other believers to pray for him. As is typically the case, his motivation is that he would be able to continue to fulfill his God-given calling. If God delivered Paul from those who sought to destroy him, his ministry would continue. In addition, the answer to such prayers would lead other believers to give thanks to God for the grace he had shown Paul. Both of these motivations are very significant for intercession, and both can be summarized under the petition, "Thy kingdom come." Paul's ability to continue in his ministry of evangelism would help the kingdom come by bringing more people into God's kingdom. The thanksgiving elicited by God's answer to the Corinthian believers' prayer is also a fruit of the kingdom of God. Thanksgiving is a vital aspect of worship (see, for example, Psalm 136) and God seeks those who will worship him in spirit and truth. Those who prayed for Paul could do so with confidence that they were praying according to God's will.

Paul also speaks in 2 Corinthians 9:12-15 of believers giving thanks to God, this time as a result of the Corinthians' financial generosity. He writes to them that "this service that you perform is not only supplying the needs of God's people but is also overflowing in many expressions of thanks to God." Because of their obedience, others will praise God. Then Paul adds that when those benefiting from the Corinthians' generosity pray, their "hearts will go out to you because of the surpassing grace God has given you. Thanks be to God for his indescribable gift!" Just as the answer to their prayers will lead others to thank God, so the Corinthians will benefit from the prayers of others because of their obedient service.

When we pray for others, we can keep the same two motivations in mind. Prayer that others are able to fulfill their God-given calling is always appropriate. And the grateful worship of God that results from answered prayer is a wonderful fruit of the kingdom of heaven.

Exercise

Take some time to review the many prayers you've written so far. Give thanks to God for all the ways he's responded to your prayers. Thank him for bringing his kingdom more fully in your life and the lives of others through your prayers. Pray also that he would enable you to fulfill your God-given calling. Thank him for hearing and responding to this prayer.

Day 23 - Paul and the Corinthians, Part 2 (2 Corinthians 13:1-10)

Paul concludes the letter of 2 Corinthians with a warning. Some in the church at Corinth have not accepted his apostolic authority and are acting in ways that go against his teaching. The Corinthian believers are "demanding proof that Christ is speaking" through Paul, who claims his power comes not from himself but through God's power in him. Paul turns the tables and challenges the Corinthians to examine themselves to see if they are truly in the faith, that is, to see if Christ really dwells in them. He then says that he prays that they would not do anything wrong. His motivation in praying this way is not that his apostolic authority would be established by their obedience, but that they would do what is right even if it looks like he's been proved wrong. He adds that his prayer is for their "perfection." The Greek word translated perfection has the sense of being made complete, put in order, restored. Thus his prayer is that the church in Corinth might experience the spiritual completeness and wholeness God intends. Paul urges the Corinthians in 13:11 to make this completeness their personal goal.

Reflection

Paul's apostolic ministry was certainly not easy. The believers at Corinth had challenged his authority, and some were living rebelliously and in a manner inconsistent with the gospel. Paul tells them he is praying that they would live right, that is, in a manner consistent with his proclamation of the gospel. God had poured out his mercy on them, and the only reasonable and appropriate response would be to live according to God's ways, as proclaimed by Paul. As an apostle, it was his privilege and responsibility to teach and shepherd believers in the faith. His motivation in praying for them is not for his own reputation, but for the Corinthians' development in Christ-like character. He prays for them to be made complete and whole. This wholeness refers to the individual person as well as the entire church. The sin of individual believers, whether pride or immorality or spiritual complacency, hurts not only the individual but also the body of Christ as a whole. Thus Paul prays that they might humbly walk in the ways of Christ, as Paul had shown them. This would lead to their restoration to the wholeness and unity God intended for them.

Exercise

Thank God that he has poured out his mercy for you, just as he did for the Corinthian believers. Then ask him to search your heart to make you aware of any ways you might not be living up to your name as a Christian. Ask him to do the same for your church. Then pray as Paul did that you and they would do what is right and be made whole in Christ. Thank God for hearing and responding to your prayer.

Day 24 - Paul and the Ephesians (Ephesians 1:1-23)

Paul's first prayer in the book of Ephesians soars to great and almost mystical heights. In the words leading up to the prayer, Paul describes the incredible blessings given to believers in Christ. We have been chosen to be blameless in God's sight, adopted as God's children, lavished with grace, redeemed and forgiven. In all these and other things, God's will is powerful, perfect and certain of fulfillment. The Holy Spirit guarantees our inheritance, and all these things serve to give glory to the God who made us his own in Christ.

Paul then writes "for this reason." The reason to which he refers is the riches that are ours in 1:3-14. Paul says his prayer for the Ephesians stems from what God has done for them. First, he tells them he has "not stopped giving thanks for you, remembering you in my prayers." The great praise Paul gave in 1:3-14 (see verse 3, "Praise be to the God and Father of our Lord Jesus Christ . . .") leads naturally now to thanksgiving that the Ephesians have enjoyed the benefits offered in Christ. Next, he asks that God may reveal himself further to the Ephesians ("give you the Spirit of wisdom and revelation"), so that they might know God more deeply. Third, he prays a related prayer, that the eyes of the Ephesians' hearts may be opened to receive the revelation that God pours out. In summary, he prays that the Ephesians might grow deeper in their knowledge of God, both through God's continued revelation of himself and through their own receptivity to that revelation.

The knowledge Paul prays for consists of three things. One is an understanding of the hope to which God has called them. This hope, described already in 1:3-14, refers to the ultimate and future goal of their salvation. Paul wants them to understand where they are headed, to a heavenly existence in which they will live with God for eternity, and where they will be made forever blameless and pure, and removed from the painful state of affairs of this present world. The second is to know the delight God has in them as his inheritance. Because they are in Christ, and God sees Christ in them, they are a glorious gift to God, who rejoices in their future life with him. Third, Paul asks that they may understand that the same power God used to raise Christ from the dead and to give him authority over all other powers in the universe, is available to them. Paul asks God that the believers in Ephesus might know God better by coming to a deeper understanding of these three things.

Reflection

It's easy to get lost in Paul's language, which moves easily between exalted praise and petition. Nonetheless, his prayer is a wonderful example of what to pray for other believers, and it is helpful to boil it down to its essence. His prayer also illustrates an aspect that is typical for Paul, namely, intercession in the context of praise and thanksgiving. Considering that Paul's letters were read to churches that were gathered for worship, the combining of thanksgiving and intercession was quite natural. The ancient church (after the time of the apostles) typically made intercession during times of giving thanks to God, which occurred after the preaching of the Word in the receiving of the Lord's Supper. In fact, the Greek word for the Lord's Supper (*eucharisteo*/Eucharist) actually means thanksgiving.

How can we boil the content of Paul's prayer down into a memorable and usable form? First, we must remember that Paul based his intercessions on the incredible work God had done on behalf of believers ("for this reason"). It is thus appropriate, before we intercede, to follow Paul's example and recall some of the many blessings God has given to believers in Christ. He has chosen us, called us, shown us grace, brought glory to himself through us, sealed us with his Holy Spirit, promised us ultimate redemption, treasured us, and given us access to his glorious power. These are all things for which we should thank and praise God. They also remind us of the standard reason for praise in the Old Testament: the Lord is gracious and compassionate, slow to anger and rich in love.

Next, Paul gives thanks for those for whom he is praying. He can do this because of the many blessings God has poured into them. He first praises God for what he offers all believers in Christ. Then he thanks God for keeping his wonderful promises specifically in the lives of the Ephesians.

Third, he prays that the Ephesians might know God better. This knowledge comes through God's own willingness to make himself known to them, and through the receptivity of their hearts. It includes deeper understanding of the very things for which Paul has already praised and thanked God. Paul lists three of these in his prayer: the rich future hope given to believers, their incredible value to God and the amazing power that is theirs in Christ. These three things, hope, value and power, are easy to remember and always appropriate to pray for other believers.

Paul's intercessory prayer pattern can be summarized as follows:

1. Praise God for all he has given us in Jesus Christ.

2. Thank God that he has also given those very blessings to those for whom we are praying.

3. Ask that God would give deeper understanding of his gracious nature (as expressed through these incredible blessings) to those for whom he prays. These blessings include great hope for the future, great value

in God's eyes and incredible power available to believers.

Exercise

Write a prayer for other believers following Paul's pattern. It might look something like this:

Lord, I praise you for all the blessings you have given to those who believe in Jesus Christ. You have shown them great grace, poured out your love for them and treated them as your special treasure, given them hope for the future and great power to live in the present through your Holy Spirit. And Lord, I thank you that you have graciously given these very things to _____, whom I lift up to you now in prayer. Please grant them a deeper knowledge of yourself. Show more of yourself to them, and give them hearts to understand who you really are. Make them more aware of the blessings you have promised them in the future. Help them to see how much you treasure them. And show them the amazing power you've given to Jesus Christ, which is also available to them. Lord, as always, thank-you for hearing and responding to my prayer. In Jesus' name, amen.

Day 25 - Paul and the Ephesians, Part 2 (Ephesians 3:14-21)

P aul again prays for the Ephesians. He begins, "for this reason I kneel before the Father." The "reason" to which he refers connects back to 3:1, where he uses the same phrase. It appears as if Paul began to pray in 3:1, then decided first to say more about God's plan for the Gentiles (3:2-13). In 3:14, he returns to his prayer. The actual reason for his prayer is in Ephesians 1 and 2. What is this reason? Paul has traced God's plan to form Jews and Gentiles together into a "holy temple in the Lord," that is, "a dwelling in which God lives by his Spirit" (2:21-22). The foundation of this building is "the apostles and prophets, with Christ Jesus himself as the chief cornerstone" (2:20). Therefore, Paul's prayer is motivated by a desire to see God's purpose accomplished in the Ephesian believers. He wants them to grow, through their relationship to Christ, into a unified community that displays the glory of God.

Paul's prayer for them centers on receiving power. He gives two important reasons they need God's power. The first is the strengthening of their "inner being." This strengthening occurs through the Holy Spirit, and has the result of Christ dwelling in their hearts through faith. The indwelling of Christ for which Paul prays is not the ongoing presence of Christ that all believers experience. Certainly the believers in Ephesus would already have invited Christ into their lives. What Paul prays for is that Christ's presence in the Ephesian believers would reach the fullness and glory God intends. As their inner beings strengthen, they will allow Christ to live through them, and thus truly become vessels of Christ. Along with this, he prays secondly that they may have power to grasp the magnitude of Christ's love for them. It is only with such an experiential understanding, which surpasses mere intellectual knowledge, that they will fulfill the purpose to which God has called them.

Paul concludes his prayer with an exalted doxology (word of praise). This doxology affirms that God is able to accomplish in us far beyond what Paul asked. It also sets Paul's intercession in the context of praise.

Reflection

This prayer of Paul's is a tremendous example to all that desire to pray for other believers. It expresses proper submission through physical posture ("I kneel"), and addresses God as the source of all the good things that his children have ("the Father, from whom his whole family in heaven and on earth derives its name"). In concludes with a doxology of praise that attributes to God the glory and honor he alone deserves. And this grateful recognition of God's character and goodness permeate the petitions Paul makes ("out of his glorious riches," "this love that surpasses knowledge," etc.).

The core of Paul's prayer is the request for power. Unfortunately, in our modern culture the word power often has negative connotations. Images of despotic rulers come to mind, or people that are willing to destroy others to assert their authority. Within the church certain sectors have so emphasized the power of the Holy Spirit, manifested through spectacular healings and the like, that many believers have rejected the association of power with the Christian faith. For Paul, however, God's power in the lives of believers is an essential element in achieving God's purpose. Central to this purpose is the formation of the church as a community of believers that radiates God's very character in the midst of this world (see again, John 17). This character includes unity, love, compassion and holiness.

The power of God for which Paul prays will have two primary effects. One is the strengthening of the inner being of believers. This is where true transformation takes place, in the heart and soul of those who follow Christ. Though we often attend to the outside and how it appears to others, it is the inner being that God is concerned with. Transformation on the inside takes place as our hearts become truly Christ's home. The title of the old leaflet, "My Heart, Christ's Home," summarizes well what Paul envisions. It is not enough to have Christ as a guest in our hearts. Paul's prayer is that he would become the owner, and put things into the order that he knows is best. It is only through God's power, mediated through the work of his Holy Spirit in our hearts and received by faith, that such an exchange of ownership can take place. As this happens, Christ's very character shines through individual believers and the church. This should be a key focus of our prayers for other believers.

The second effect of God's power working in our lives is a deeper comprehension of Christ's love. Such love cannot be understood simply on the intellectual level, though many do try to limit it in this way. We must also experience it, and when we do, it will defy description because of its magnitude. Only when believers gain such an experiential understanding will they be able to fulfill the purpose to which God has called them. This purpose, as we have seen, is to be formed into a temple of praise to the very God who loves them.

Exercise

Write a prayer modeled on Paul's prayer in Ephesians 3:14-21. Your prayer should include the following elements:

1.   A statement to God that you know his purpose is to form believers into a community that draws the world's attention to his wonderful character.

2.   Prayer that God would accomplish this purpose in those for whom you pray. Pray that out of his immeasurable resources, and through his Holy Spirit, he might supply power to other believers, so that:

      a.   They might have the faith to allow Christ to become more fully the owner of their hearts;

      b.   They would have a deeper understanding in both their minds and hearts of Christ's incredible love for them.

3.   Praise God that he is more than able to fulfill the very purpose he has set out.

Your prayer might look something like this:

> *Father, you have created the church to be a witness to your glory here on earth. In order for the church to do this, it desperately needs your help. Please supply the church with your power, Lord, power that is infinite and beyond our understanding. Give us power that changes us on the inside, so that your Son Jesus Christ would truly be the master of our hearts. Give us power to know in our hearts, as well as our minds, the immeasurable love your Son has for us. Lord, only in this way can we, the church, fulfill the purpose to which you have called us. Lord, you are more than able to do all that we ask, and to do more than we can even imagine. We give you all the praise for what you have done, are doing and will do to manifest your character through the church. In Jesus' name, amen.*

Day 26 - *The Ephesians' Prayer for Paul (Ephesians 6:10-20)*

Paul here urges the Ephesians to be "strong in the Lord and in his mighty power." This exhortation is clearly reminiscent of his prayer for them in 3:14-21. The power of which he writes includes putting on the Lord's armor, since the fight of faith is not against other people but against spiritual powers and authorities. Paul paints a picture of this armor, describing the belt of truth, the breastplate of righteousness, the gospel of peace that protects the feet, the shield of faith, the helmet of salvation and the sword of the Spirit (the word of God). He then exhorts them to "pray in the Spirit on all occasions with all kinds of prayers and requests." They are to be alert and praying continuously for other believers.

Paul then specifically requests prayer for his ministry. He asks that God would give him courage and the words to speak as he proclaims the gospel. After stating that he is imprisoned for doing this very thing, he asks again that he may be fearless in declaring God's truth.

Reflection

Paul here sets intercessory prayer in the broader context of spiritual battle. The existence of a spiritual realm is assumed, as is the ongoing conflict between God's purposes (which will in the end prevail) and the destructive activities of evil spiritual forces. Paul urges the Ephesians not to limit their perspective to the natural realm, for the battle they are in is truly cosmic in scope. In order to be successful, they must learn to wield the tools of the spiritual realm. These include God's truth, righteousness, the gospel, faith, salvation and the word of God. In addition, they must be praying in the Spirit. Paul emphasizes the inclusive and continuous character their prayers should possess, with all kinds of prayers and requests being prayed always on all occasions for all the saints.

What does Paul mean by praying "in the Spirit?" He means a number of things. Broadly speaking, Paul wants us to pray with the spiritual realm in mind. If the battle we are fighting is spiritual and not material, then our prayers must reflect this. And certainly God's purpose as described by Paul, to see believers built into a temple of glory to God, is a spiritual purpose. It is not enough to pray for a good place for our church to meet, for a kind congregation, for a friendly pastor, etc. Paul's vision for the people of God, which is also God's vision, is about a fundamental spiritual transformation that will bring believers true fulfillment and attract a world hungry for such reality. Thus, to pray in the Spirit is, at the very least, to pray with God's spiritual purposes in mind.

We can see the contents of such a prayer in Paul's own request. He asks to be made fearless in proclaiming the life-changing gospel. He also asks that God would give him the words to speak to those who hear. Significantly, Paul does not ask to be set free from the physical constraints of imprisonment. He does, however, ask to be set free from the spiritual constraints of fear and inability to communicate God's truth. Thus Paul's own prayer is focused clearly on the spiritual purposes of God.

But there is another aspect to praying in the Spirit. As Paul and others make clear, only believers in Christ are indwelled by the Holy Spirit. Paul has already told us that one of the Holy Spirit's functions is to intercede for believers "with groans that words cannot express" (Romans 8:26). This is a great benefit, since we are weak and do not know how to pray as we should regarding these weaknesses. So how does the Spirit help us? Certainly it would be wonderful enough if the Spirit simply prayed independently of us and on our behalf. Yet Paul's exhortation for us to pray in the Spirit is naturally connected to this intercessory ministry of the Spirit. Many believers have experienced times when they were impressed to pray for someone else unexpectedly. Such impressions are a way the Spirit can help us in our weakness, in this case our finitude, to be aware of needs for prayer in the spiritual realm. For believers who pray in a spiritual language (tongues), the idea of groans that words cannot express makes perfect sense. Paul himself says that those who speak in tongues speak to God in a way that others cannot understand, and that they speak "mysteries in the Spirit" (1 Corinthians 14:2 (NRSV)). Such prayer is made not with the believer's mind but with his spirit (1 Corinthians 14:15). Thus, praying in tongues is likely a means by which believers can cooperate with the Spirit's intercessory ministry.

Paul alludes to such Spirit-directed prayer in Ephesians 5. Here he exhorts the Ephesian believers:

> Be filled with the Spirit. Speak to one another with psalms, hymns and spiritual songs. Sing and make music in your heart to the Lord, always giving thanks to God the Father, in the name of our Lord Jesus Christ. (5:18-20)

Our words to God are to flow out of our hearts in song and music, with constant thanksgiving in Jesus' name. Not only that, but the Spirit's filling should lead us to talk to one another in new ways as well, with psalms, hymns and spiritual songs.

What we must keep in mind is that prayer is a key weapon in the kingdom of God. This kingdom is not a physical kingdom built with human hands, but a spiritual kingdom built by our humble cooperation with God's own Spirit. It is impossible to pray the way Paul describes without the involvement of God's Holy Spirit. Our goal as intercessors should be to learn to co-operate with the Spirit as effectively as possible.

Exercise

Thank God that he has provided you with armor to fight battles in the spiritual realm. Thank him also that he has invited all believers to join him in building his kingdom through the use of this armor. Pray that God will give you a deeper understanding and experience of what it means to pray in the Spirit. Ask the Spirit to help you in your weakness to pray according to the will of God. Ask also that the Spirit would help you to understand how to pray continuously. Thank God for hearing and responding to your prayer.

Day 27 - Paul and the Philippians (Philippians 1:1-11)

P aul wrote this letter, like Ephesians, while he was in prison. As with his letter to the Ephesians, he tells the Philippians of his joy and thanksgiving for what God is doing in their lives. He also expresses his confidence that God will bring to completion the work he has begun in them. Paul's affection for them is obvious, and he freely expresses his longing to see them.

Once again, he states clearly just how he prays for his readers. He asks that God would help their love to abound in knowledge and depth of insight. This growth in a love marked by wisdom is not an end in itself, but will enable them to discern what is best. The ultimate goal (the "and" after "best" is added by the NIV and gives the wrong impression this is the second of two goals) of such discernment is that they might be pure and blameless when Christ returns, bearing eternal, spiritual fruit through their relationship with Christ. All of this accomplishes God's purpose of glorifying himself through the church.

Reflection

Paul's prayer here is another great example of praying for others according to the priorities of God's kingdom ("Thy kingdom come"). Love is an obvious Christian virtue, but Paul prays for a love that is wise, perceptive and aware of God's truth. Such a love moves high above much of what the world calls love, which is often aimless and self-gratifying. The development of such godly love (1 Corinthians 13 paints a great picture of what such love looks like) will have the result of increased discernment about how the Philippians should live their lives. Daily choices regarding use of money, time, talents and energy will move toward what is best, rather than what is simply acceptable. The Philippians will thereby grow in purity and blamelessness, fulfilling their God-given calling to be a manifestation of his very character here on earth.

Perhaps what is most striking about this prayer is that Paul desires the Philippians to view their lives as a continuous journey towards Christ-likeness. He has already spoken in 1:6 of the good work God has begun in them, which he will also bring to completion. His describes his own life as a constant pressing onward toward the fulfillment of his God-given calling (3:10-14). Thus Paul assumes and prays for progress and growth in the Christian life, rather than a static contentment with the way things are. This is the life he lives, and his prayer is that the Philippians would experience the same.

Commentators have rightly called Paul's prayer here a prayer for revival. In a sense, all of Paul's prayers are prayers for revival. Revival involves inner change that bears external fruit. Inner change occurs as Christ is formed more fully in us (see Galatians 4:19). The fruit of this formation includes love of God and others, holiness, heart-felt worship and unity of focus on the things of Christ. Our prayer then, following Paul's example, is that God would indeed bring to completion the wonderful work of revival he has begun in us. Like Paul, we must commit to pray for such change and then expect that God hears and responds to our prayers.

Exercise

Thank God that he is the one who will bring to completion the good work he has begun in believers. And thank him that he takes seriously your prayers toward that end. Then pray for God to revive the hearts of those in your church. Follow the pattern of Paul's prayers, which typically move from the inside out. Inner revival (in our hearts) is what leads to external fruitfulness. Start with your pastor(s), and pray also for other church leaders, and then pray through the names in a church directory. A good way to do this is to write a prayer such as Paul's, then ask God to apply it to each person you name. Then simply speak or write to God the names for which you want to pray. In this way, you can pray the same thing for a great number of people. And remember: the Spirit is interceding with you. Make note of any names that, when you write or speak them, you sense may need special prayer. And ask the Spirit to help you intercede in an appropriate way for those people. Thank God for hearing and responding to your prayer.

Your prayer might look something like this:

Lord, I want to pray for my church today. Please give each person who is a part of our body a love that is increasingly full of knowledge and insight, so that they may better discern and follow what is truly best for them and those around them. Jesus, let this growth constantly lead our church towards the kind of purity and blamelessness that you yourself exhibited while you were on earth. We want to be filled up with your character, individually and together, when you return, so that the Father is glorified through us. Help each one that I now name. Lord, I bring before you _____, _____, _____, etc. Thank you, Lord, for hearing and responding to my prayer. In Jesus' name, amen.

Day 28 - Paul and the Colossians (Colossians 1:1-14; 4:2-4)

Paul also wrote the letter to the Colossians while in prison. Unlike Ephesians and Philippians, however, Paul had neither started nor visited the Colossian Christians. He begins his letter in a familiar way, telling the Colossians he always gives thanks to God when he prays for them because of the work God is doing in them. Epaphras, he writes, had taught them well, and informed Paul of their wonderful progress.

He then writes "for this reason," just as he did in Ephesians 1:15, 3:1 and 3:14. As in those cases, the reason Paul prays is also the very thing for which he was giving thanks: God was doing a mighty work of transformation in them. Having thanked God for their progress, he boldly asks that they might continue to grow. He asks God to fill them with knowledge of God's will "through" (or, "which is") all spiritual wisdom and understanding. The result of such knowledge will be that they live lives worthy of Christ, pleasing him in every way. Such lives will be marked by the fruit of good works, deepening knowledge of God, power for godly endurance and patience, and an attitude of thanksgiving to God. Paul then reminds them of what they are to be thankful for. God graciously brought them into his kingdom, rescuing them from the dark domain of Satan. He redeemed them and forgave them through his Son, Jesus Christ.

Reflection

It is hard to get around the fact that Paul has priorities in his prayers that are fundamentally spiritual! This very fact is both an encouragement and a challenge to us. Paul illustrates for us what the mature Christian's focus in intercessory prayer (and all prayer) should be, namely, that

God's character would shine through his people. In each of his prayers so far, Paul has used different language to express essentially this same point. Here in Colossians 1, the focus is on a divinely given knowledge of God's will.

What does Paul mean by God's will? It is easy to limit our understanding of God's will to the things that concern our future and happiness. For example, we are encouraged to pray for God's will regarding our vocation, marriage partner, living place, etc. Sometimes we will also pray for God's will concerning our church home, or the other believers God brings into our lives. Paul's understanding of God's will is much broader and more encompassing than this. For example, in 1 Thessalonians 4:3 he writes, "It is God's will that you should be sanctified." And in the second chapter of the same book, he exhorts his readers, "Be joyful always; pray continually; give thanks in all circumstances, for this is God's will for you in Christ Jesus" (5:16-18). We could give many more examples, but it should be clear that, for Paul, God's will has to do primarily with our own growth together in Christ-likeness.

Thus, when Paul prays that God would fill the Colossian believers with the knowledge of his will, he is asking that they might understand the purpose for which God created and called them. It is obvious as well that this understanding is not simply intellectual awareness, but a knowledge that leads to transformation. He says that he prays for this knowledge "in order that" the Colossians would live in a manner worthy of and pleasing to Jesus Christ. This is another way of saying in very personal terms what Paul has consistently said, that his prayer for believers is for growth in Christ-like character. Here he equates this character with good works, knowledge of God, patient endurance in trials and persecution, and thankfulness. He invites them to pray for him in a related manner, that God would open a door for the gospel and that he could proclaim it clearly. Such proclamation is, of course, the first and necessary step to bringing others into Christ-like character.

Prayers such as Paul prays here require time for fulfillment. For this reason, perseverance is required to continue praying this way. Paul himself urges the Colossians to "devote" themselves to prayer, being watchful and thankful (4:2). Prayers such as the one in Colossians 1:9-14 can and should be prayed continually for other believers. In this way, they serve as a constant spiritual weapon against the deceptions and inducements of the evil one.

It is significant that Paul goes directly from his prayer for the Colossians into an extended description of the glory of Jesus Christ. This hymn of praise to Christ affirms both the divinity and the humility of the one for whom the Colossians are called to live. It also shows once again how easily Paul moves from praise and thanksgiving to petition and back again. In this Paul is a great example to us, in that our prayers for others should be made in the context of thanksgiving and praise for what God does.

Exercise

Begin praying today by thanking God for all that he has done to bring you into his family, and to give you an eternal and wonderful purpose. Then pray that God would deepen your understanding of his will. Pray also that your priorities, both in how you live and how you pray for others, would be increasingly more in line with his will. Pray that your deepening understanding of his will would lead you to live a life more worthy of, and pleasing to, the one who called you, Jesus Christ. Pray that Jesus might so live in and through you that he does good works through you, helps you to know God better, gives you patient endurance in the trials and temptations of this life, and gives you a deep sense of thankfulness at all times. Ask finally that God would give you the strength and faith to pray this prayer regularly, not only for yourself but also for others. Thank him for hearing and responding to your prayer.

Day 29 - Paul and the Thessalonians (1 Thessalonians 1:1-3; 2:17-3:13)

The letter of 1 Thessalonians was written long before Paul wrote Ephesians, Philippians and Colossians. It fact, it may be the first biblical letter he wrote. Acts 17-18 describe the historical context of this letter. Paul had preached for a few weeks in Thessalonica, which is in modern day Greece. When some Jews instigated persecution against Paul and Silas, the two were sent away to Berea for their own protection. The same men who had stirred up dissent in Thessalonica then came to Berea, and Paul was sent to Athens, leaving Silas with Timothy in Berea. Timothy eventually joined Paul in Athens, and was sent back to Thessalonica. Paul moved on to Corinth, where Silas and Timothy eventually joined him. It is generally believed that Paul wrote 1 Thessalonians from Corinth.

It should not surprise us now that Paul's letters are always full of thanksgiving. This was the life of Christ shining through him, and he begins this letter by telling the Thessalonians of his constant gratitude to God in his prayers for them. They were a model to believers elsewhere (1:6-10), receiving the gospel joyfully in the midst of great persecution (2:13-16). Paul describes in passionate terms his deep desire to return to them, and the efforts he had made to do so. They are his glory and joy, because they had responded positively to the gospel. But Satan had stopped him from visiting them, so he sent Timothy to strengthen and encourage them in their new faith. Paul was concerned that they might have fallen into temptation in the midst of the great persecution they were suffering. Timothy, however, brought back a glowing report of their faith and their steadfastness, and for this Paul says he cannot sufficiently give thanks to God.

Paul then tells the Thessalonian believers how he is praying for them. He prays that he might see them again, in order that he might "supply what is lacking in your faith." He also prays that Christ would make their love increase and overflow, as does Paul's love for them. He asks that God would give them inner strength so that they would be made ready for the return of their Lord, that is, that they would be made blameless and holy.

Reflection

What is most striking about Paul's prayer for the Thessalonians is not its content. We have already seen these themes in his prayers, with their focus on God glory manifested through the Christ-like growth of believers. What is striking is the passionate concern Paul had for his flock in Thessalonica. And what this illustrates for us is that intercessory prayer is often driven by relationships with those for whom we pray.

Paul had spent only a few weeks with the Thessalonians, and for some of this time they were undoubtedly seekers rather than believers. Yet the bond Paul developed with them through his ministry among them was truly rich. And what motivated him the most was a sincere concern for their spiritual well-being. What if wolves came in and wrecked their faith? What if they gave up in the face of persecution? Paul aches to return to them, and to do what he can by God's grace to strengthen and encourage them.

This kind of compassionate fervor comes more easily to some of us than others. Yet it is apparent that intercession and relationship go hand in hand. It is much easier to pray for those for whom we care deeply. Since Paul was a missionary who preached the gospel to unreached peoples and helped establish churches in their midst, it was natural for him to become attached to those he helped. However, it seems today that believers are often encouraged to keep "professional distance" between themselves and those to whom they minister. Such an approach looks wise, but flies in the face of the passionate concern Paul exhibited. This is not to say that Paul had an unhealthy attachment to the Thessalonian believers. On the contrary, he does not long for them so that he can feel important and needed. Instead, he demonstrates a deep concern for their spiritual welfare. This healthy concern is the same that was demonstrated by Jesus in his dealings on earth. One notable example is his love for Mary, Martha and Lazarus described in John 11. This was not a love driven by Jesus' own needs, but one that flowed out of his God-centered heart.

It is a good thing to pray for ourselves, that we would develop hearts that can love others with the kind of fervor demonstrated by Paul. As this happens, our prayers for others will be more and more motivated by love instead of a sense of obligation.

Exercise

Thank God that he is a God who delights in relationship with people. Ask that he might give you a heart like his in this area, one that is people-oriented in a healthy way. Ask him to search your heart and reveal any ways in which you relate to others to fulfill your own needs. Confess whatever he brings to mind, and receive the forgiveness that is yours in Christ. Then ask God that he would change your heart to be a heart like Paul's, one that prays for others out of a deep concern for their well-being. Thank God for hearing and responding to your prayer.

Day 30 - Paul and the Thessalonians, Part 2 (2 Thessalonians 1:1-12; 2:13-3:5)

Paul here writes again to the young Thessalonian church. As is his custom, he begins by expressing his thanks to God for these believers (and telling them so). Their faith is growing and their love for one another is increasing, and Paul boasts to other churches of their patient and persevering faith. He is confident that they will continue to endure persecution and thus show themselves worthy of God's calling (that is, live up to what God has graciously called them to be), and that those who trouble them will be judged. With these things in mind, Paul prays constantly for them. He asks that God may count them worthy of their calling, and that God would supply power to his purpose in them. His motivation in these prayers is that Jesus Christ would be glorified in them, and they in Christ, all by the grace God supplies. Their glorification in Christ refers to the fulfillment of their calling to become holy and blameless, fully Christ-like in character (see Romans 8:29-30).

In chapter 2, Paul again gives thanks to God for the Thessalonians. This time he focuses on how God chose them and saved them through his Spirit's work, and through their faith. He also prays for God's encouragement and strengthening to continue in them, as manifested in their words and deeds.

Finally, Paul asks the Thessalonians to pray for him. Paul's burden is for the success of the gospel. He asks them to pray that it would spread rapidly and be received by others as they had received it. He prays that they would be delivered from those who do not have faith, and expresses his confidence that God will protect them. He also affirms his confidence that they will obey his teaching, and that the Lord will guide them into God's love and Christ's perseverance.

Reflection

Paul's consistency in intercessory prayer should now be quite apparent. He always gives thanks to God for what he has accomplished in the believers for whom Paul prays. He then asks God to continue this work of transformation, and to bring it ultimately to completion. His focus is always on Christ being formed in the believers, and he is motivated by a concern for God's glory.

When he asks prayer for himself, the pattern is the same. He has thanked God for his gracious work in the Thessalonian believers. Now he asks that God would do similar work among the others to whom he preaches. His central motivation is the increase of God's glory, not his own.

Paul is committed to this pattern of prayer, a pattern we too should follow. We can, like Paul, follow thanksgiving for what God has done in those for whom we pray with prayer for God's continuing work in them, so that God may be glorified. He also consistently encourages those for whom he prays, by telling them both how he thanks God for them and how he prays for them.

Exercise

Thank God for his continuing work of making you more like Christ. Then ask God to bring to mind a person or group for whom you have been praying, and to whom you will write a letter. In the letter, tell them how you thank God for what he has done in their lives. Be as specific as possible, listing the types of things Paul typically does, such as increased love, perseverance in trials, and faith. Then tell them how you are praying for continued growth in these very qualities, so that God will be glorified in them. Thank God for hearing and responding to your prayer.

Day 31 - Paul and Timothy, Part 1 (1 Timothy 2:1-8; 2 Timothy 1:1-18)

T he letters of 1 & 2 Timothy differ from the other letters of Paul that we have read, because they are written to an individual rather than a church. Timothy had accompanied Paul on some of his missionary journeys, and was the shepherd of the church at Ephesus. In his letters to Timothy, Paul gives instructions regarding prayer that range from general to specific and from impersonal to personal.

In 1 Timothy 2:1-8, Paul instructs Timothy with respect to some practical matters of church worship. He exhorts the gathered body of believers to pray for other believers by asking God to give them rulers who allow them to live peaceful, quiet, godly and holy lives. He says that such governance is good and pleasing to God, since it promotes the saving of many people. He describes the work of Jesus Christ as a mediator between God and men, and states his own calling to bring the gospel to the Gentiles. He then expresses his desire that men in the church would pray with the lifting up of their holy hands and without dissension.

In 2 Timothy 1 Paul turns to two much more personal prayer matters. First, he reports that he gives thanks to God for Timothy's faith. Then in verse 18, he states his request that Timothy show mercy to Onesiphorus (mentioned also in 4:19) and his household, because of the help he showed Paul in prison.

Reflection

These letters put a slightly different spin on Paul's typical intercessory concerns. His request that the church pray publicly for those in authority is motivated by a concern for the furtherance of the gospel. With benevolent governance, many more will hear the gospel, and believers will be able to live out their faith unhindered. He exhorts the men of the church to pray together with hands lifted. This was a common posture for prayer in the ancient church, and is associated with both prayer and praise in the book of Psalms (63:4; 134:2; 141:2). Jesus used a similar posture when he blessed his followers before his ascension (Luke 24:50). Raised hands may have indicated both reverence for and humble receptivity to God.

Both of Paul's prayers in 2 Timothy are for individuals. He is thankful for God's transforming work in Timothy, an attitude we have come to expect in Paul's prayers. For Onesiphorus he simply asks for mercy from God, because he had shown mercy to Paul. Both these prayers illustrate that what we have learned from Paul's corporate prayers apply also to his prayers for individuals.

Exercise

Thank God that he desires all people everywhere to be saved. Ask him to establish rulers in your country who will allow believers to live in peace and to proclaim the gospel without hindrance. Pray similarly for other countries that you know to be difficult for the gospel, such as communist or Islamic countries. For guidance in how to pray for believers in these countries, try visiting web-sites such as www.persecution.com (*Voice of the Martyrs*) and www.persecutedchurch.org (*International Day of Prayer for the Persecuted Church*). Thank God for hearing and responding to your prayer.

Day 32 - Paul and Philemon (Philemon)

This is the last of Paul's letters in the New Testament, and also his shortest. Paul is writing once again from prison. He addresses Philemon as a friend and fellow worker, and appeals to him to treat his returning (and perhaps runaway) slave Onesimus as a brother in Christ.

Paul characteristically begins his letter by expressing the thanks he gives to God as he prays for Philemon. He has heard of Philemon's faith in Christ and his love for other believers. His prayer is that Philemon would actively "share" his faith. It is wrong to take the phrase "sharing your faith" in the limited sense of verbally witnessing to others. It refers more broadly to Philemon's faith being expressed (that is, shared - the Greek word is *koinonia* – see the same idea in Hebrews 13:16) in his actions. This expression of his faith will lead Philemon to experience full awareness of all the good that is his as a believer in Christ. This good likely includes the virtuous acceptance of Onesimus as a brother in Christ (see verse 14). In verse 22, Paul also refers to Philemon's prayer for Paul's return. Paul expresses expectant hope that he will indeed be a guest of Philemon's.

Reflection

Once again, Paul follows the pattern of giving thanks for what God has done, then praying for God to continue his work. As in his letters to Timothy, Paul here applies this pattern to his prayer for an individual. As always, he not only thanks God for the ones to whom he writes, but also tells them of his thankfulness. Through this purposeful encouragement, he likely hopes to motivate his reader(s) to heed his exhortations. The prayer he prays for Philemon is that his faith might be "shared" with others, in particular as Philemon gently receives his runaway slave Onesimus. Paul's prayers, as always, seek kingdom ends; disunity between Philemon and Onesimus would be detrimental to the body of Christ.

It is important to notice that Paul's exhortations to Philemon do not evade the truth of the situation. It is easy for us to think of unity, and the love it requires, in soft and sentimental terms, as if unity is simply a good feeling toward others in the body. Biblical unity is much more costly. It requires speaking the truth in love, confession of sin, and a willingness to work through painful and long-term tensions and misunderstandings. However, such unity is not only God's expectation of us but also the means by which we will show the world we are his disciples.

Exercise

Thank God that in the Trinity of Father, Son and Holy Spirit he has shown us what true unity looks like. Then ask him to bring to mind some believers who are struggling with one another. Thank God for the work he has already accomplished in them. Then ask that God might give them strength to accept each other, so that they can experience more fully the good that God intends. Pray also that they might both be able lovingly to speak the truth in order to restore unity. Thank God for hearing and responding to your prayer.

Day 33 - Prayer in the Letter to the Hebrews (Hebrews 13:15-21)

We do not know who wrote the letter known as Hebrews. Whoever it was concludes with a list of exhortations to his audience. Believers are told to offer God sacrifices of praise and good works. They are to obey their leaders so as not to make their leaders' task burdensome. The author then asks his audience to pray for him and his companions, who have a clear conscience and desire to live honorably. Like Paul, the author desires to see his readers again, and he asks them to pray for this.

The author also prays a blessing on his readers. He asks that the God of peace who, true to his promise, raised Jesus their shepherd from the dead, would equip them with every good thing for doing God's will. He also asks that God would work in him and his companions what is pleasing to God, through Christ. Like Paul, he ends with a doxology of praise to Christ, "to whom be glory for ever and ever. Amen."

Reflection

Having read so many of Paul's prayers, we can see the continuity between what Paul prayed and what this author prays. Though Paul's characteristic emphasis on thanksgiving is not obvious in this passage, it is in the rest of the book of Hebrews, which in a real sense is an extended thanksgiving for what God has accomplished in Christ for those who believe. The author's desire to visit his readers is highly reminiscent of Paul's letters, as is the emphasis on God supplying what is necessary for doing his will and pleasing him. It is always fitting to conclude our prayers with praise, and the author of Hebrews offers a sacrifice of praise and exhorts his readers to do the same (13:15, 21).

Exercise

Take time to review your prayer on Day 19 of the New Testament journey, when you studied Romans 1:1-17. In the exercise for that day, you took time to lay your deepest desires before God, and asked him to fulfill them and remove desires he has not given. Write down how God has responded to these prayers. Do you have a desire, like Paul and the author of Hebrews, to encourage a particular person or group through your presence? Has God clarified your desires, and used them to help you pray with greater purpose? Thank God that he hears and responds to your prayers. Close by offering him praise, speaking or singing a favorite psalm (Psalm 145 is a good one) or song of praise.

Day 34 - Prayer for Healing (James 5:13-20)

James here gives practical advice on what to do in three common but different human situations. He has already warned his readers about complaining about each other (5:9) and making oaths (5:12). Then he offers some positive alternatives to these negative forms of speech. When in trouble we should pray. When happy we should sing God's praise. And when sick, we should ask the elders of the church to pray over us and anoint us with oil in Jesus' name. Such prayer, offered in faith, will bring healing from the Lord, including the forgiveness of sins. James then notes the importance of making others aware of our weaknesses so that we may pray for one another and experience healing. Elijah is an example of a man who demonstrated the effectiveness of a righteous person's prayers.

Reflection

Prayer for healing of physical illness is a natural and biblical act of faith. Jesus often healed physical as well as spiritual illness while he was on earth. As intercessors, we can still bring those in need of healing to Jesus for his help. The anointing with oil is a powerful symbol of God's healing presence, as it was during Jesus' earthly ministry. Mark writes in his gospel of the twelve disciples, "They drove out many demons and anointed many sick people with oil and healed them" (6:13). Why call the elders, or spiritual leaders of the church? It may be that the sickness in view is severe enough that the one needing prayer does not have the strength to pray. In this case, the elders are viewed as a trustworthy source of faithful prayer, though others could perhaps be effective as well. What is essential though is neither the oil nor the elders, but faith in Christ. We are to offer such prayers in the name of the Lord, and James goes to great lengths to extol the importance of faith in the God whom we call Lord. Just as with Jesus' earthly ministry, forgiveness of sins and physical healing go hand in hand. This is not because all physical illness is the immediate and direct result of some specific sin. Rather, all physical illness and suffering are in a more general way related to the power of sin, to which the world is currently enslaved. Jesus came to bring freedom from this enslavement, physical healing and the forgiveness of sin being two primary means by which this freedom comes.

It is making too much of this passage to press it to say that prayer offered in faith will always result in physical healing. We have seen before that such a view actually limits God's freedom, treating him an impersonal force subject to our manipulations. However, it should be clear that believers are to pray for physical healing, placing their faith in their Lord, Jesus Christ, who was and is the great healer. As we persist in faith that God does heal, God may surprise us in the wonderful ways he does hear and respond to our prayers.

Exercise

Prayer for the sick is an important biblical practice. When God brings physical healing, it provides testimony to his existence, power and character. Are you willing to pray in person for one who is sick? Are you willing to join with other believers in anointing such a person with oil? If you presently know of someone who is struggling with physical illness, consider how you can pray for them in person. If they are in the hospital or a care facility, this will require visiting them there. When anointing with oil, which is a symbol of the Holy Spirit, simply dip your finger in some olive oil or specially purchased anointing oil, and make a cross on the person's forehead. Begin your prayer by stating that you are praying in the name of the Father, the Son and the Holy

Spirit. Then pray boldly that God will heal the person, because he is merciful and has here in James 5 shown that he is willing and able to heal. Thank him aloud for hearing and responding to your prayer. Be sure to write down just what you did and said, and to continue to pray for this person.

Day 35 - John's Vision and the Prayers of the Saints (Revelation 5:1-14; 8:1-5)

In this final book of Scripture, John the apostle gives us a highly symbolic picture of God's ultimate victory over the spiritual forces that seek to destroy his kingdom. Specifically, in chapter 5 he describes a powerful scene in which the Lamb of God, Jesus Christ, is found to be the only one worthy to open a scroll held in God's right hand and sealed with seven seals. When the Lamb takes the scroll, the four living creatures and the twenty-four elders, which continually worship around the throne of God, fall down before him, just as they had done before God himself (see 4:6-11). The deity of the Lamb is thereby affirmed. Each living creature and elder has a harp and is holding a golden bowl full of incense. The bowls of incense are said to be the prayers of the saints. The creatures and elders then sing three new songs of praise to the Lamb of God. In the second song the myriad of angels joins them, and in the third the chorus increases to include "every creature in heaven and on earth and under the earth and on the sea, and all that is in them." When the creatures say "amen," the elders fall down and worship the Lamb.

Chapters 6-8 describe the significance of the seven seals that sealed the scroll. Each one represents judgment against the enemies of God, with the seventh seal issuing in a new series of seven trumpets. In chapter 8, when the seventh seal is opened, an angel stands before the throne of God and offers incense there with the prayers of the saints. In 6:10-11 the souls of those who had lost their lives for their faith cry out for God, asking him once and for all to set things right, bringing judgment on those who had killed God's people.

Reflection

The intensity and power of these scenes are incredible. It is easy to get caught up and even lost in the details. However, there is much to be gained from stepping back and taking in the overall picture. It is clear from this glimpse into the spiritual realm that creation itself is oriented like a compass needle towards the throne of God. John describes various types of beings, and they all have in common their worship of God. When the Lamb enters the picture, the beings accord him the same worship as God himself, implying (as we have already noted) that he is not simply a great being but himself divine. The Lamb initiates the final judgments on those who have rejected God's kingdom. At the beginning and end of the seven seal judgments the prayers of the saints are mentioned, and in the midst of these judgments the souls of those martyred cry out for vindication. The saints' prayers likely included cries for the vindication of God's chosen ones.

What is the significance of these cries for vindication? In a nutshell, what these souls are asking is for God's kingdom finally to come. Jesus described the coming of God's kingdom as a radical reordering of the status quo. The weak would become the strong, the poor would become the rich, prisoners would be set free and the first would be last. Though this reordering had begun with Jesus' first coming, its full and complete effect would not be seen until the end of the age. What John describes in the book of Revelation is the final culmination of the coming of the kingdom of God. Of necessity this included a humbling of those who had chosen to exalt themselves against Jesus by seeking to destroy the people of his kingdom. So the prayer for vindication seen here is a call for the final dividing lines to be drawn between those that are for God's kingdom and those that are against it. Jesus himself alluded to this in Luke's gospel when he told the parable of the persistent widow. He summarizes the parable with these words: "And will not God bring about justice for his chosen ones, who cry out to him day and night? Will he keep putting them off? I tell you, he will see that they get justice, and quickly" (Luke 18:7-8).

What is even more significant for our purposes, however, is the integral connection between worship and prayer seen in these passages. In chapter 5 in particular, each elder and living creature holds both the prayers of the saints and a harp (representing the new song of praise sung to the Lamb). The elders and other creatures then sing songs of praise that give glory to the Lamb of God. After the opening of the seals and the description of their judgments, the prayers of the saints go up before God and another series of judgments begins. We have already seen that these prayers consist of cries for God's kingdom to come, so that God would vindicate his persecuted people. They are intercessory prayers in the truest sense.

This connection between praise and intercession throughout Scripture is by now familiar to us. Proclaiming God's character is a form of praise, and many of the intercessory prayers we've examined have done this. Paul's prayers for others typically begin with thanksgiving, which is another form of praise. And prayers such as Solomon's in 1 Kings 8 clearly set intercession in the context of exalting God. For this reason, it is essential that intercessors make it a habit to begin their prayers with praise and thanksgiving. This is true when we pray alone, and just as vital when we join together in prayer with God's people. Like Jesus said, and as John describes here in the book of Revelation, will not God then see that they get justice, and quickly?

Exercise

Imagine that you, like the four living creatures and the twenty-four elders, have a harp in one hand and a bowl of incense in the other. The harp represents your songs of praise to Jesus Christ, the Lamb of God to whom the Father has given all authority and dominion over creation for eternity. The bowl represents your prayers, especially those for other believers who have suffered because of their faith in the Lamb. Now lift up the harp to the Lord. Do this by writing out and saying or singing the three new songs in Revelation 5:9-13. Then pray to God as the martyred saints did. Write out their prayer in your own words: "How long, Sovereign Lord, holy and true, until you judge the inhabitants of the earth and avenge the blood of those who suffer for you?" Thank him for hearing and responding to your prayer.

Continuing the Journey

Continuing the Journey

C ongratulations! You have completed a long and challenging journey through Scripture. On this journey you have encountered many people just like yourself. These people sometimes show wonderful faith, and other times seem oblivious to what God is doing. Sometimes they act in obedience, and other times they have hard, rebellious hearts. Sometimes they demonstrate patient waiting, and other times they are presumptuous and bull-headed. Just like you, they are real people with ups-and-downs, successes and failures, good qualities and bad. Just like you, God uses them in spite of their weakness.

Our goal on this journey has been to focus on a particular aspect of our life as believers, namely praying for others. As you have seen, praying for others has a long and rich history in the bible. This is because God has given us, his treasured creatures, a key role to play in bringing about his good purposes on this earth. God is the sovereign ruler over creation, and nothing can thwart his wise and good purposes. At the same time, in his sovereignty he has chosen to give us ways to affect the achievement of his purposes. Prayer is one such way. Through vital conversation with God, we learn more of him and express our praise, thanksgiving, confession, and concerns to him. As we express our concerns for others, the Lord responds according to his character and promises, transforming us as well as the ones for whom we pray. These changes bring glory to God, for they give us character more like his, and allow us to show others more effectively what God is really like.

The role we play is one of mediation. As intercessors, we stand between God and others, bringing their needs to

God, and God's blessings to them. God's Holy Spirit guides us as we pray, and helps us to see the world through God's eyes rather than with our own limited sight. As we learn to trust God's character and promises and to respond to his leading, we grow in faith, making us more effective as intercessors. We learn that intercession takes place most naturally in the context of thanking God for who he is and what he has done. Ultimately, we become better God-glorifying worshipers even as we pray.

It is important to realize that although the *Journey into Intercession* is completed, the real work of intercession lies ahead. It is time to apply all that you have learned and experienced along the way to a life of prayer for others. As you do, God will continue to shape your faith, to guide and direct your thoughts, and to grow his own character in you. He will also bring glory to himself by responding to your prayers in ways beyond your comprehension. All of these things will motivate you to pray more. Perhaps most motivating, however, is the deep, intimate, and fulfilling relationship with God that will develop as you pray. It is just such a relationship that marked the lives of those men and women we have studied. And it is just such a relationship that God wants to have with you.

Endnotes

[1] Walter Brueggemann in Patrick D. Miller, ed., *The Psalms and the Life of Faith* (Philadelphia: Fortress, 1995), 137.

[2] Hans Schönweiss & Colin Brown, "Prayer," in *The New International Dictionary of New Testament Theology*, vol. 2 (Grand Rapids: Zondervan, 1975), 873.

[3] Douglas V. Steere, *Dimensions in Prayer* (New York: Harper and Row, 1962), 77.

[4] Dallas Willard, *Hearing God* (Downers Grove, IL: InterVarsity, 1999), 35.

[5] Leanne Payne, *Restoring the Christian Soul: Overcoming Barriers to Completion in Christ through Healing Prayer* (Grand Rapids: Baker, 1991), 183-190.

[6] Leanne Payne, *The Healing Presence: Curing the Soul through Union with Christ* (Grand Rapids: Baker, 1989), 89.

[7] F. B. Meyer, *Our Daily Walk* (Scotland: Christian Heritage, 1993), January 12.

[8] "Awake My Soul," 2002 Same Old Dress Music (Admin. by Music Services).

Scripture Index

Genesis
12:1-3 17
12:3 3
16 16
17 17-10, 19
18 3, 22-23, 35
18:10-15 18
18:16-33 20-22
20 23-25
24 26-27
25:21b 26

Exodus
8:1-15, 20-32 28-30
8:10 28
9:13-35 28-30
9:29 28
10:1-20 28-30
12:43-49 83
15:24-25 31-33
17:1-7 31-33
19 5
19:3-6 58
19:5-6 4
19:8 34
20:6 40
25-31 34
32 91
32:1-14 34-36
32:4 34
32:10 35, 47
32:14 105
32:15-35 37-38
32-34 47
33:17 40
33-34 39-41
34 105
34:6-7 48, 118

34:8 40
34:9 41

Leviticus
5:17-19 93
13:4-6 45
19:18 113

Numbers
9:4-14 83
11 8, 42-44
11:19 47
11:20 42
11:29 8, 42
12 45-46, 49
12:3 46
12:8 46
13 47
14 47-48
14:11 47
16 49-51
16:3 49
16:48 49
20:1-13 55
21 52-53
21:4-9 52-54
27:12-23 55-56

Deuteronomy
9:23-24 47
9:25-29 47

1 Samuel
2 84
2:12-17 57
2:18-26 57-59
2:20 57
12:6-25 60-61

2 Samuel
12 62-63
24 64-66
24:14 64
24:25 64

1 Kings
8 206
8:22-63 69-71
8:51, 53 69
17 77
17:7-24 72-73
18:16-40 74-75

2 Kings
4:8-37 76-77
6:8-23 78-79
13:1-6 80-82
18:1-4 53
18:5-8 80
18:12 80
19:9-20, 35-37 80-82
19:20-34 80

1 Chronicles
21 64-66
29 69
29:10-13 68
29:10-17 67
29:10-22 67-68

2 Chronicles
6:12-7:6 69-71
7:3 69
29:1-31:1 83-85
29:27-30 83
30:9 83
30:20 83

30:27 83
32:79 80

Ezra
8 86-87
8:21-23 86
8:22 86

Nehemiah
8:3 89
9 88-90
9:16-18 90
9:32 88

Job
1-2 91
38 91
40:1-6 91
42 5
42:7-17 91-92

Psalms
1 20
20 107-10
23 53
32 20
32:10 21-22, 26
34 154
61:6-8 107-10
63:4 195
72 107-10
103 70
118 154
122 107-10
134:2 195
136 166
141:2 195
145 199

Isaiah
37 80
52:13-53:12 93-
95, 119

53:4 119, 121
53:12 93, 119-20
59:1-3, 20-21 94
59:15b-16 93

Jeremiah
7:16 96
11:14 96
12:1 97
12:1-17 96-98
12:5-13 96
12:14-17 96
14:11-12 96
15:1 96
18:19-23 97
25:11-12 103
42 99-100

Daniel
2:1-23 101-02
2:47 102
9 103-04

Joel
2:28-32 43

Jonah
1 105-06
4:2 105-06

Micah
3:1-3 96

Matthew
1:1-17 24
5:43-48 113-15
5:48 113
6:5-13 116-18
6:14-15 117
7:7-12 120
8:5-17 119-21
9:35-10:1 122-23

9:1-8 124-25
9:18-26 126-27
15 2
15:1-28 84
15:21-28 77
15:21-31 128-29
17:14-19 130-32
17:20-21 130
20:17-19 133
20:20-28 133-34
20:25-28 134

Mark
1:29-34 119-21
2:1-12 124-25
2:29 130
5:21-43 126-27
6:13 201
7:24-37 128-29
8:22-30 135-36
9:14 10
9:14-28 130-32
9:22 130
9:29 130-31
10:32-34 133
10:35-45 133-34

Luke
5:17-26 124-25
6:27-36 113-15
6:36 113
7:1-10 119-21
8:40-56 126-27
9:37-42 130-32
10:1-11 122-23
10:9, 11 122
11:1-4 116-18
11:13 146
17:6 130
18:7-8 206
22:24-27 133-34
23:24 143
23:34 5, 114

List of Works Consulted

Anderson, Bernhard W. *Out of the Depths: The Psalms Speak for Us Today*, rev. ed. Philadelphia: Westminster, 1983.

Brodie, Thomas L. *The Gospel According to John: A Literary and Theological Commentary*. New York: Oxford, 1993.

Brown, Colin, ed. *The New International Dictionary of New Testament Theology, vols.* 1-4. Grand Rapids: Zondervan, 1975-78.

Bruce, F. F. *The Book of Acts*, in *The New International Commentary on the New Testament*, ed. F. F. Bruce. Grand Rapids: Eerdmans, 1986.

_____. *The Epistle to the Hebrews*, in *The New International Commentary on the New Testament*, ed. F. F. Bruce. Grand Rapids: Eerdmans, 1964.

Brueggemann, Walter. *The Psalms and the Life of Faith*, ed. Patrick D. Miller. Philadelphia: Fortress, 1995.

Carson, D. A. *A Call to Spiritual Reformation: Priorities from Paul and His Prayers*. Grand Rapids: Baker, 1992.

_____. *The Sermon on the Mount: An Evangelical Exposition of Matthew 5-7*. Grand Rapids: Baker, 1978.

_____, Douglas J. Moo and Leon Morris. *An Introduction to the New Testament*. Grand Rapids: Zondervan, 1992.

Daniélou, Jean. *Prayer: The Mission of the Church*. Transl. David Louis Schindler, Jr. Grand Rapids: Eerdmans, 1996.

Davids, Peter. *Commentary on James* in *The New International Greek Testament Commentary*, eds. W. Ward Gasque and I. Howard Marshall. Grand Rapids: Eerdmans, 1982.

Davies, J. G., ed. *The New Westminster Dictionary of Liturgy and Worship*. Philadelphia: Westminster, 1986.

Deiss, Lucien. *Springtime of the Liturgy: Liturgical Texts of the First Four Centuries*. Collegeville, Minnesota: The Liturgical Press, 1979.

Enns, Peter. *Exodus* in *The NIV Application Commentary*, ed. Terry Muck. Grand Rapids: Zondervan, 2000.

Fretheim, Terence E. *Exodus*, in *Interpretation*, ed. James L. Mays. Louisville: John Knox, 1991.

Gaebelein, Frank E., ed. *Genesis, Exodus, Leviticus, Deuteronomy,* in *The Expositor's Bible Commentary,* vol. 2. Grand Rapids, Zondervan, 1990.

_____. *Matthew, Mark, Luke,* in *The Expositor's Bible Commentary,* vol. 8. Grand Rapids: Zondervan, 1984.

_____. *Hebrews, James, 1, 2 Peter, 1, 2, 3 John, Jude, Revelation,* in *The Expositor's Bible Commentary,* vol. 12. Grand Rapids: Zondervan, 1981.

Guthrie, Donald. *The Pastoral Epistles,* in *The Tyndale New Testament Commentary,* ed. R. V. G. Tasker. Grand Rapids: Eerdmans, 1957.

Lewis, C. S. *Letters to Malcolm: Chiefly on Prayer.* San Diego: Harcourt, 1964.

Marshall, I. Howard. *Luke: Historian and Theologian.* Grand Rapids: Zondervan, 1970.

_____ *Acts,* in *Tyndale New Testament Commentaries,* ed. R. V. G. Tasker. Downers Grove, Illinois: InterVarsity, 1980.

Martin, Ralph P. *Worship in the Early Church.* Grand Rapids: Eerdmans, 1964.

Miller, Patrick D. *Interpreting the Psalms.* Philadelphia: Fortress, 1986.

Morris, Leon. *The Gospel According to John,* in *The New International Commentary on the New Testament,* ed. F. F. Bruce. Grand Rapids: Eerdmans, 1991.

Motyer, J. Alec. *The Prophecy of Isaiah: An Introduction and Commentary.* Downers Grove, Illinois: InterVarsity, 1993.

Mounce, Robert H. *The Book of Revelation,* in *The New International Commentary on the New Testament,* ed. F. F. Bruce. Grand Rapids: Eerdmans, 1977.

Newsome, James D., Jr., ed. *A Synoptic Harmony of Samuel, Kings, and Chronicles.* Grand Rapids: Baker, 1986.

Payne, Leanne. *Listening Prayer: Learning to Hear God's Voice and Keep a Prayer Journal.* Grand Rapids: Baker, 1994.

_____. *Real Presence: The Glory of Christ With Us and Within Us.* Grand Rapids: Baker, 1995.

_____. *Restoring the Christian Soul: Overcoming Barriers to Completion in Christ through Healing Prayer.* Grand Rapids: Baker, 1991.

_____. *The Healing Presence: Curing the Soul through Union with Christ.* Grand Rapids: Baker, 1989.

Peterson, David. *Engaging With God: A Biblical Theology of Worship.* Grand Rapids: Eerdmans, 1992.

Sailhamer, John. H. *The Pentateuch as Narrative: A Biblical-Theological Commentary.* Grand Rapids: Zondervan, 1992.

Saliers, Donald E. *Worship as Theology: Foretaste of Glory Divine.* Nashville: Abingdon, 1994.

Schmemann, Alexander. *The Eucharist: Sacrament of the Kingdom.* Transl. Paul Kachur. Crestwood, New York: St. Vladimir's Seminary Press, 1987.

Senn, Frank C. *Christian Liturgy: Catholic and Evangelical.* Minneapolis: Fortress, 1997.

Sheets, Dutch. *Intercessory Prayer.* Ventura, California: Gospel Light, 1997.

Steere, Douglas V. *Dimensions in Prayer.* New York: Harper and Row, 1962.

_____. *Prayer and Worship.* Richmond, Indiana: Friends United Press, 1988.

Wall, Robert W. *Revelation,* in *New International Biblical Commentary,* vol. 18. Nashville: Broadman & Holman, 1991.

Wallace, Ronald S. *The Message of Daniel,* in *The Bible Speaks Today,* ed. J. A. Motyer. Downers Grove, Illinois: InterVarsity, nd.

Webber, Robert E. *Worship Old and New: A Biblical, Historical, and Practical Introduction,* rev. ed. Grand Rapids: Zondervan, 1994.

White, James F. *Documents of Christian Worship: Descriptive and Interpretive Sources.* Louisville: Westminster/John Knox, 1992.

Willard, Dallas. *Hearing God.* Downers Grove, Illinois: InterVarsity, 1999.

About the Author

Eric W. Bolger (PhD, Trinity Evangelical Divinity School) is professor of philosophy and religion and chair of the division of humanities at College of the Ozarks in Point Lookout, Missouri. He is an adjunct faculty member at the Robert E. Webber Institute for Worship Studies in Orange Park, Florida, from which he earned the Doctor of Worship Studies degree. He also serves as the Staff Elder for Harvest Evangelical Free Church in Branson, Missouri, where he regularly preaches.

Printed in the United States
90088LV00007B/34-48/A